Controversies in psychology

Psychology studies people and the way they behave. Some findings inevitably challenge existing moral, political and religious beliefs, leading to heated debate. *Controversies in Psychology* examines these debates, particularly those about control and manipulation, and perceived differences between one group of people and another.

Philip Banyard is Associate Senior Lecturer in Psychology at Nottingham Trent University and a Chief Examiner for A level Psychology.

Routledge Modular Psychology

Series editors: Cara Flanagan is the Assessor for the Associated Examining Board (AEB) and an experienced A-level author. Kevin Silber is Senior Lecturer in Psychology at Staffordshire University. Both are A-level examiners in the UK.

The *Routledge Modular Psychology* series is a completely new approach to introductory level psychology, tailor-made to the new modular style of teaching. Each short book covers a topic in more detail than any large textbook can, allowing teacher and student to select material exactly to suit any particular course or project.

The books have been written especially for those students new to higher-level study, whether at school, college or university. They include specially designed features to help with technique, such as a model essay at an average level with an examiner's comments to show how extra marks can be gained. The authors are all examiners and teachers at the introductory level.

The *Routledge Modular Psychology* texts are all user-friendly and accessible and include the following features:

- practice essays with specialist commentary to show how to achieve a higher grade
- chapter summaries to assist with revision
- progress and review exercises
- glossary of key terms
- summaries of key research
- further reading to stimulate ongoing study and research
- website addresses for additional information
- cross-referencing to other books in the series

Also available in this series (titles listed by syllabus section):

ATYPICAL DEVELOPMENT AND ABNORMAL BEHAVIOUR

Psychopathology
John D. Stirling and Jonathan S.E. Hellewell

Therapeutic Approaches in Psychology
Susan Cave

BIO-PSYCHOLOGY

The Physiological Basis of Behaviour: Neural and hormonal processes
Kevin Silber

States of Awareness
Evie Bentley (forthcoming)

COGNITIVE PSYCHOLOGY

Memory and Forgetting
John Henderson

Perception: Theory, development and organisation
Paul Rookes and Jane Willson (forthcoming)

COMPARATIVE PSYCHOLOGY

Reproductive Strategies
John Gammon (forthcoming)

DEVELOPMENTAL PSYCHOLOGY

Early Socialisation: Sociability and attachment
Cara Flanagan (forthcoming)

PERSPECTIVES AND RESEARCH

Ethical Issues in Psychology
Mike Cardwell (forthcoming)

Introducing Research and Data in Psychology: A guide to methods and analysis
Ann Searle

SOCIAL PSYCHOLOGY

Social Influences
Kevin Wren (forthcoming)

Interpersonal Relationships
Diana Dwyer (forthcoming)

STUDY GUIDE

Exam Success in AEB Psychology
Paul Humphreys

OTHER TITLES

Health Psychology
Anthony Curtis (forthcoming)

Sport Psychology
Matt Jarvis (forthcoming)

Controversies
in psychology

Philip Banyard

London and New York

First published 1999
by Routledge
11 New Fetter Lane, London EC4P 4EE

Simultaneously published in the USA and Canada
by Routledge
29 West 35th Street, New York, NY 10001

Typeset in Times by Routledge
Printed and bound in Great Britain by Clays Ltd, St Ives plc

British Library Cataloguing in Publication Data
A catalogue record for this book is available from the British Library

Library of Congress Cataloging in Publication Data
Banyard, Philip, 1953–
Controversies in psychology / Philip Banyard.
p. cm. – (Routledge modular psychology)
Includes bibliographical references and index.
I. Title
II. Series.
BF121.B285 1999
150–dc21   98–35362

ISBN 0–415–19496–2 (hbk)
ISBN 0–415–19497–0 (pbk)

Contents

Illustrations

Figures

Tables

Acknowledgements

Phil Banyard would like to acknowledge the help of Nelson Mandela, the cast of *Frasier*, and Nookie Bear in the preparation of this text. He would like to but can't because he has never met any of them. He does, however, acknowledge the helpful comments from Matt Jarvis, his colleagues Mark Shevlin, Mark Griffiths, Mark Davies and other members of the Noor Jahan discussion group, Lesley Phair, and also his parents for encouraging him to have an opinion and express it.

The series editors and Routledge acknowledge the expert help of Paul Humphreys, Examiner and Reviser for A-level Psychology, in compiling the Study Aids section of each book in the series.

They also acknowledge the Associated Examining Board (AEB) for granting permission to use their examination material. The AEB do not accept responsibility for the answers or examiner comment in the Study Aids section of this book or any other book in the series.

The author and the publishers would like to thank all the copyright holders of material reproduced in this volume for granting permission to include it. Every effort was made to contact authors and copyright holders, but if proper acknowledgement has not been made, the copyright holder should contact the publishers.

Introduction

Controversies in psychology

Control
Giving psychology away
Perceived differences between people
Human nature
Social Darwinism
The controversy
End note

What are controversies? I guess there is a controversy whenever there is more than one point of view. So, for example, I might think that the Village People were one of the musical giants of the twentieth century, but you might not agree. We have a controversy. If we take this approach into psychology then we will find that everything is controversial, because for every piece of evidence that is put forward, there are a number of interpretations of that evidence. Psychology, and all other sciences, develop through debate and controversy. It is a part of how they operate. In the context of this book, however, the term controversy has a special meaning.

Some arguments and debates have an extra edge, perhaps because of the consequences of the debate or because they challenge people's core beliefs. In psychology, there are some issues that can have a very serious effect on our daily lives and so have been the centre of fierce debate. For example, labelling people as intelligent or unintelligent can have lifelong consequences. Psychology also looks at why people behave in the way they do and makes some suggestions about what is human nature. This inevitably challenges some people's moral, political and religious beliefs. It is these debates that we will look at in this text. The underlying themes of these controversies centre around the control and manipulation of people, the perceived differences between one group of people and another, and our beliefs about human nature.

Control

Who controls whom? If psychology achieves its ambitions and is able to describe and affect the behaviour of people, then who should be allowed to control whom? Say, for example, we find a way of changing people's attitudes and behaviour very effectively; should we use this to stop young people from starting to smoke cigarettes? This would have a long-term benefit because it would improve their health and reduce the amount of money they spend on drug consumption. This all sounds like a good idea, but what about if we then use the same technique to encourage people to attack minority groups?

The **behaviourist** J.B. Watson suggested that the aim of psychology was to develop a technology that can control people. For example, in his 1924 book *Behaviourism*, he wrote:

> The interest of the behaviorist in man's doings is more than the interest of the spectator – he wants to control man's reactions as physical scientists want to control and manipulate other natural phenomena. It is the business of behavioristic psychology to be able to predict and to control human activity.
>
> (Watson, 1924, p. 11)

The ability to be able to predict and control my own behaviour is very useful. I will be able to choose how to act rather than to react unthinkingly to changes in my environment. The ability to predict and control someone else's behaviour, on the other hand, raises a number of ethical and moral issues. So it is important to know how psychological information will be used and who will use it on whom. Watson is clear on who should have the information:

> If psychology would follow the plan I suggest, the educator, the physician, the jurist and the businessman could utilise our data in a practical way as soon as we are able, experimentally to obtain them.
>
> (Watson, 1913, cited in Shotter, 1975, p. 32).

This view was endorsed by B.F. Skinner in his book *Beyond Freedom and Dignity* (1972). In this, he argued that we need to develop a technology of behavioural control to improve conditions in our societies. For example, he wrote:

> The real issue is the effectiveness of techniques of control. We shall not solve the problems of alcoholism and juvenile delinquency by increasing the sense of responsibility. It is the environment which is 'responsible' for the objectionable behaviour, and it is the environment, not some attribute in the individual which must be changed.
>
> (Skinner, 1972, pp. 76–7)

Skinner believed that our behaviour is moulded by our environment rather than motivated by our personal values and beliefs. According to Skinner, the reason I behave well or badly is not because I am a good or bad person but because of the reinforcements and punishments I have experienced in my life. Therefore, my bad behaviour is not my fault and I can stand up in court and say 'society is to blame, Your Honour'. If you follow this argument through, then you end up with Skinner's suggestion that we need more control in our society rather than less. That control should be used to give people the **reinforcements** and punishments that encourage good behaviour (whatever that is).

A similar point of view was put forward by the British psychologist Hans Eysenck, who wrote:

> The problem to be discussed is: how can we engineer a social consent which will make people behave in a socially adapted, law-abiding fashion, which will not lead to a breakdown of the intricately woven fabric of society.
>
> (quoted in Heather, 1976, p. 46)

Eysenck is arguing that psychology should be on the side of the state to maintain the status quo, whatever that is. If psychology adopted this position then it would be used to resist social change, which usually comes about through dissent and political action. The ethical question for psychology is whether it should be used by governments to control people and create an ordered society, or whether it should be used to enhance personal freedoms. There is no obvious answer to this, and the question has to be struggled with by each new generation of scientists.

Giving psychology away

A different point of view to the above was put forward by George Miller (1969) in his Presidential Address to the American Psychological Association. Miller pointed out that according to its constitution the object of the American Psychological Association is to promote human welfare. But what does this mean? Whose welfare is being promoted, and at whose expense? He said:

> I believe that the real impact of psychology will be felt, not through the technological products it places in the hands of powerful men, but through its effects on the public at large, through a new and different public conception of what is humanly possible and humanly desirable.

> (Miller, 1969, p. 1067)

> Understanding and prediction are better goals for psychology and for the promotion of human welfare because they lead us to think, not in terms of coercion by a powerful elite, but in terms of the diagnosis of problems and the development of programmes that can enrich the lives of every citizen.

> (Miller, 1969, p. 1069)

> Our responsibility is less to assume the role of experts and try to apply psychology ourselves than to give it away to the people who really need it.

> (Miller, 1969, p. 1070)

Miller suggested a very different aim for psychology from that suggested by Watson, Skinner and Eysenck. I guess it is for the reader to decide which side they have greater sympathy for, though for my part, I would endorse the general sentiments of Miller, and I have a lot of concerns about any attempts to use psychology to control and manipulate the general population, even when it may appear to be 'for their own good'.

The issue of control is one that will continue to occupy the attention of psychologists. You will see as you read through this text that psychology has often not been on the side of the angels. It has been used, for example, to manipulate our consumer behaviour (see Chapter 3 on advertising), it has been used as a weapon in the arguments of scientific racists (see Chapter 4 on bias, and Chapter 5 on psychometric testing), and it has been used in warfare (see Chapter 1 on war, and Chapter 2 on propaganda).

Psychology has also been used to achieve a lot of positive changes, but not surprisingly, these changes are not so controversial, and so do not get much coverage in this text. I would not want the reader to get the impression that the bulk of psychology is an exercise in exploitation conducted by an army of deranged and amoral scientists. This text, however, aims to look at the controversies in the subject and so concentrates on the more disturbing aspects of psychological research.

Perceived differences between people

This section is titled 'perceived differences ...' rather than just 'differences between people', for a good reason. The controversial part of psychology is not so much how people differ, but what differences they are thought to have. On the whole, it is only possible to make very broad generalisations about differences between groups of people and the variation within the group is often much greater than the difference between the groups (see Chapter 4 on bias).

If we want to make statements about the differences between people, we need to be able to take reliable and valid measurements of psychological variables. We also need to have a clear theoretical understanding of what we are measuring (these issues are discussed in Chapter 5 on psychometrics). If we want to go further and make statements about differences between groups of people, then we need to be able to define the groups of people, and have measurements that can be applied to all people (these issues are discussed in Chapter 4 on bias). For example, if we take the issue of cultural diversity, it is not possible to put everybody, or indeed most people, in a neatly defined cultural group. Think of this from your own point of view, what cultural and subcultural groups do you feel you belong to?

The most worrying aspect of looking for differences between groups of people is the political consequences of this work. These consequences derive from a genetic explanation of the difference. If an individual or group of people are defined as being inferior to other people, and it is suggested that this inferiority is caused by their genetic make-up, then one response to this will be to discourage these people from having children.

Human nature

What is **human nature**? The question turns around the characteristics of human behaviour that are due to genetic programming and which characteristics are due to our social environment. It can be suggested that behaviour that is largely under genetic control cannot be adjusted through social interventions such as education, whereas behaviours that are largely under social control are open to greater adjustment. This situation masks a much more complicated state of affairs, and therefore a much more complicated argument. It is obviously part of our nature to breathe, and also to eat. Without these two behaviours we die very quickly. However, the act of eating, though a biological requirement for survival, is also under a lot of social control. The way that we eat, the things we choose to eat, where we choose to eat them and who we choose to eat with, are all aspects of eating that vary from person to person, and culture to culture. It is in our nature to eat, but the way we eat is modified by social influences. Already, then, the question of human nature has become a little debatable.

Philosophers have proposed theories about human nature since they first sat on a rock to think. The seventeenth-century philosopher Thomas Hobbes wrote:

bellum omnium contra omnes

which roughly translated from the Latin, means that all people will kick seven bells of hell out of each other if they are given the opportunity. Hobbes believed that it is in human nature to be competitive, to fear other people and to have a desire for glory, and that warfare is biologically inevitable.

The scientists of the Victorian era in the nineteenth century developed a biology of social class. They believed that the differences in achievement between people were largely due to breeding, and that the poor and the uneducated were biologically inferior. Some of the consequences of these views are discussed in other parts of this text (Chapter 4 on bias, and Chapter 5 on psychometrics). It is perhaps worth making a short diversion into the principles of natural selection to see how they believed this breeding works. According to Darwin's account of evolution, natural selection is the way that species change over time and become more adaptive to their environment. The key features of this argument are:

- every generation has too many individuals
- some survive and some die
- the genetic characteristics of the survivors are retained
- the genetic characteristics of the dead are lost

What this means is that the features that help some individuals to survive are likely to be passed on to the next generation. The species then develops through a process of selective breeding – selected by the environment. This can work for behavioural characteristics as well as physical characteristics.

Social Darwinism

A number of scientists (who appear later in this text) believed that much of human behaviour is under genetic control and has developed through the forces of natural selection. They noticed that better health care and social conditions meant that not so many people were dying at a young age and they feared that the effect of natural selection was being blunted. In other words, if the weak survive then they will pass on their weak genes to the next generation, They proposed that instead of allowing the environment to selectively breed the better members of the species, this selection should be taken on by people. This selective breeding (**eugenics**) of a superior class of people could then be used to improve society and remove people who, for example, do not put the top back on a tube of toothpaste once they have used it. Although I make light of this approach, it had some powerful supporters who put forward views that make our hair stand on end today. For example, Francis Galton wrote:

> There exists a sentiment for the most part quite unreasonable against the gradual extinction of an inferior race.
>
> (Galton, 1883; cited in Rose *et al.*, 1984, p. 30.)

It is now clear that it is not possible to fully explain the development of human behaviour using these principles, but the sentiments have found a new home in the modern theory of **sociobiology**. This theory (for example, Wilson, 1975; Dawkins, 1976) attempts to explain our behaviour using genetic principles and produces entertaining, plausible, though fundamentally flawed accounts (for a review of sociobiology see Hayes, 1995). It is not appropriate in this text to launch into a critique of sociobiology, though it is worth noting that the debate between supporters (not me) and opponents of sociobiology generates a considerable amount of heat.

The controversy

When we consider human nature, there is an academic controversy about (a) which characteristics are most affected by genetics, (b) how much they are affected by genetics, and (c) how much we can adapt our behaviour in response to personal and social demands. The reason that this debate generates so much heat is because the view of human nature we choose will lead us to certain solutions to the perceived problems of society. If, for example, we believe that violent and criminal behaviour is due to genetic features of the individual, we might try and deal with it by surgical attacks on the brains of violent criminals or through the sterilisation of offenders. The practical and ethical problems with this solution means that it is not at the front of modern debate, but it is a logical development from the arguments of social Darwinism and sociobiology.

So where does this leave us in our debate about human nature? My suggestion (and I hasten to add that I do not claim this to be original) would be that human language gives us a good model for examining human behaviour. It would appear that there are a number of biological features that structure human language. For example, there are specific brain sites for key features of language comprehension and production. There also appear to be a number of universal features of all languages, and this suggests some form of genetic structure to the way we develop this skill. However, there are hundreds of different languages in the world, and we are able to use language in an infinite number of ways, for a wide range of purposes. I would argue that our biology provides us with a range of abilities and opportunities, but the way we develop them and choose to use them is affected by our social development and our personal interpretation of the world.

End note

Psychology is inevitably controversial because it attempts to interpret and explain human behaviour and experience. We will not like everything that we find out about ourselves, and we will not agree with all the interpretations made of the evidence. In this text, I have tried to present a number of controversial issues in a way that allows the reader to develop their own opinion on them. I do not, however, pretend to be without bias, and I have strong opinions about most of the issues covered in the next five chapters. You will not need to be a rocket scientist to spot my biases, though you might like to consider whether other psychologists also have biases and whether you can spot them in their writings.

Review exercise

Have an opinion

To take part in a controversy you have to have an opinion. Start with an everyday opinion and start a controversial argument. Try the following on a family member or friend:

I think white bread is brilliant because ...

Then move up to a controversial issue in current affairs, for example:

I think nuclear power is brilliant because ...

Finally, move on to a psychological controversy and pick an argument with your teacher, for example:

I think it is human nature to (fill in some outlandish behaviour) because ...

This exercise will help you develop some idea of what a controversy is as well as helping you to deal with potentially aggressive and abusive confrontations.

1

Psychology and warfare

Introduction

War! What is it good for? Well, I guess it must be good for something because it has been part of human societies since they first appeared. It appears to be an inevitable part of human behaviour because whatever time in history you choose to look at, there will be armies marching across some part of the world in an attempt to gain control over another group of people or another territory. It is also fair to say, however, that living peacefully is another inevitable part of human behaviour, and societies spend much more time at peace than they do at war. Most people in the Western world have enjoyed a relatively peaceful existence for the last fifty years or more. We have been able to negotiate serious political difficulties in such a way that large armies have not been mobilised and our countries have not been invaded or attacked. It is possible to argue that this has only been achieved by exporting our disputes and conducting them in other parts of the world, but that argument is not really the subject of this text.

The experience of war over the last fifty years has brought us to a point where Western peoples regard war as a specialised activity carried out by expert soldiers with high-tech weapons in a place far away from their own countries. We therefore tend to see war as a dramatic event much like a film, rather than a personal event with real danger for ourselves or our families and property. This is not how warfare was conducted in the past, nor how it is conducted in most parts of the world today. For many people, warfare is a potential threat to their personal safety.

Over the last fifty years the Western viewer has been shown images of war that are either amusing (*Dad's Army*, *It Ain't Half Hot Mum*), or heroic (*A Bridge Too Far*, *The Great Escape*, *The Guns of Navarone*). For most people who experience war, however, it is neither amusing nor heroic. It is made up of frightening events, mass death, mass injury, the loss of loved ones and the loss of property and homes. On 1 July 1916 during one day at the Battle of the Somme in the First World War (1914–18) over 20,000 British troops were slaughtered due to the tactics of their commanders (Taylor, 1963). The troops were required to come out of their trenches carrying heavy equipment and charge towards the enemy trenches where they were cut down by machine gun fire. Not content with this, the tactic was repeated the next day, and for the next four months until the battle was finally brought to end with no obvious strategic advantage but at the loss of 420,000 British casualties. By the end of this war, around one-quarter of all British men of military age were casualties. It is not possible to convey in this text the horror of war and its consequences. We will, however look at some of the contributions (good and bad) that psychology has made to our understanding of war and the conduct of war.

The three questions we will look at in this chapter are:

- What can psychology tell us about warfare?
- How has psychology been used in warfare?
- What can psychology tell us about the effects of war?

What can psychology tell us about warfare?

Are we born to start wars or do we learn to do this? What is it about people that leads us into conflicts that are resolved with mass destruction and mass death? We might start by observing that aggression is an important part of our behaviour and that this attribute has considerable survival value. Aggression, however, is not war. Animals can be aggressive to each other, but most of them do not organise into groups to wage an aggressive campaign on another group of the same species. A number of psychologists have looked at the issue of warfare and offered theories about it. In this section we will briefly look at contributions from William James, William McDougall, Sigmund Freud, John Bowlby and Margaret Mead. The list reads like a Who's Who in the history of psychology, and their contributions give a flavour of the range of ideas that have been put forward to explain this very human activity.

The Williams (James and McDougall)

William James and William McDougall were both influential psychologists working in the early years of the twentieth century. They had very different political beliefs and these were reflected in their contributions to the topic of war. James was a pacifist and was therefore opposed to all forms of warfare. McDougall, on the other hand, believed in eugenics and so favoured the development of genetically superior people through selective breeding.

In James's essay 'The Moral Equivalent of War', he set out his analysis of war and how it can be avoided. This essay was written before the First World War (1914–19) at a time when this conflict was becoming inevitable and when politicians were talking about having a 'war to end all war'. James pointed out how war makes history, and that it is largely described in terms of heroic events even though it is often irrational and far from noble. Early descriptions of warfare, for example those of the Ancient Greeks, tell of pirate wars of incredible brutality. Groups of men fought for the spoils of another city or island and if they won, they plundered the goods and murdered or enslaved the inhabitants. By the turn of the twentieth century, the fight for goods and people was not seen as an adequate justification for war and different arguments were used. One argument that is still used today is that we have to go to war in order to get peace.

James suggested that wars bring some benefits and he argued that we have to find an equivalent to war that brings about the same benefits. He argued that the military values of strength, bravery, discipline and collective action are the foundation of any successful enduring society. His suggestion of a substitution for war was a mass mobilisation of young men to carry out physical labour and public works for a set number of years. This would encourage all the perceived virtues of military service without war. This view implies that people have certain qualities that have to be addressed though physical action and struggle, and without this struggle our society will become vulnerable to attack from outside and from within.

William McDougall's view was not so different in some respects. In his account of 'The Instinct of Pugnacity', he also argued that we are predisposed towards fighting. He argued that it is an important feature in the development of human beings, and he put forward the evolutionary argument the fittest survive and the weakest are removed. He suggested that this is the main reason that we fight, rather than for possessions or for ideals. He illustrated his argument with anthropological evidence of peoples who go to war but take no spoils from the war.

The solution that McDougall proposed is very different from the one suggested by James. McDougall saw warfare as an important aid to the development of a healthy society. He argued against the liberal idea that an advanced society will find other ways of resolving conflict than through war. Again using anthropological evidence, he suggested that amongst the peoples of Borneo it is the groups who were most warlike that had the superior societies. He saw evidence for this in their bigger and cleaner houses, and their stronger and braver behaviour. He therefore saw the removal of war as a dangerous development that would lead to the degeneration of our society. He therefore argued for natural selection to be re-introduced through another means, that of selective breeding where the fittest and best (presumably including McDougall himself) have more children and the weakest and the worst (fill in the list to your taste) are discouraged from breeding or killed.

The argument for a eugenic solution attracted a lot of support across Europe and the USA during the 1920s and the 1930s. It was taken to its logical and horrific conclusion by the Nazis in Germany during the 1930s until their final defeat in 1945. They dealt with the eugenics issue by murdering people they perceived to be inferior or weak, including the Jews, Slav and Gypsy peoples, homosexuals and the mentally ill.

The psychoanalysts

Freud's thoughts on war are summarised in a letter he wrote to Albert Einstein as part of an academic exchange on the subject. It was written in 1932 when the horror of the killing fields of the First World War were still having an effect on the way people thought and acted. In the letter, Freud pointed out that aggressive behaviour by one strong individual can only be challenged through collective action. A community can come together and overthrow a tyrant, though it will only avoid a new tyrant if the community stays together and is well organised. These communities can be aggressive towards each other, and this is the basis of warfare.

Freud argued that some wars have a positive effect because they establish large empires. In our recorded history, these empires have often imposed order within their boundaries and provided a peaceful existence for their citizens. There are sometimes, however, a few unfortunate down sides to large empires, such as the persecution of minorities and the suppression of civil liberties. Freud wondered whether the development of international organisations would allow nations to develop a world order that removed the rationale for warfare. At the time he was writing the League of Nations (an early version of the United Nations) was attempting, unsuccessfully as it happened, to do just that. Freud suggested that such an organisation needed to have a supreme court and also enough force to enact its judgements. It was on the second point that the League of Nations failed.

Freud believed that human beings have two basic instincts: the instinct to conserve and unify, and the instinct to destroy and kill. He suggested we might see these as the opposing forces of love and hate. He believed that we cannot suppress our aggressive tendencies, so we must divert them if we are to avoid continual conflict. He also believed that it is possible to divide people into those who are leaders and those who are led. The led 'constitutes the vast majority: they need a high command to make decisions for them, and to which they for the most part offer an unqualified submission' ([1993]1985, p. 359). He argued that we should, therefore, try to educate 'an upper stratum of men with independent minds' ([1933]1985, p. 359) to guide the masses. These independent thinkers needed to channel all their energies into rational thinking even if it involved the loss of any emotional attachments. Freud seems to be arguing that we will develop as people by becoming less influenced by our emotional side and more guided by rational thought. He believed that rational thought will turn us all into pacifists as we grasp the horror of warfare.

John Bowlby put forward another psychoanalytic explanation in an article, written with E.F.M. Durbin, in 1938. Bowlby and Durbin observed that aggression and warfare have been observed in most cultures and at most times of history. They also observed that warfare and aggression form a far smaller proportion of activity than does co-operation. They argue that warfare is just an extension of aggressive behaviours shown by individuals. The primary causes of these behaviours are identical in adults to the causes in children and also animals. The primary causes are to do with:

(a)	possession	owning property and territory, taking property and territory, and defending it;
(b)	frustration	negative feelings when ambitions and desires are blocked;
(c)	arrival of strangers	often associated with fear;
(d)	attack of a scapegoat	picking on the weak and the outsider.

These four causes are seen as the root of all aggression whether it is between individuals, or groups or even nation-states.

Durbin and Bowlby went on to point out how the defence mechanisms of psychoanalytic theory can be used to explain the features of modern human conflict. For example, fears and hatreds that exist within a group of people can be projected on to a despised group. In this way, the nation-state can show all the aggressive behaviours of an individual.

Although Durbin and Bowlby believed that war is a chronic social disease, they did not believe that this disease was incurable. They pointed out that most nations spend far more time in peaceful and co-operative activities than they do at war. The problem then is to strengthen and develop these peaceful impulses and behaviour. It also seems possible that societies can be adjusted so that the people in them do not develop so much aggression.

The anthropologist

Margaret Mead wrote extensively about the customs and behaviour of different peoples around the world. She argued that warfare is not inevitable and not part of our nature, but a human invention (Mead, 1940). She argued that many institutions such as marriage are almost universal amongst peoples, but we must have originally lived without marriage and then at some point invented it. She suggested the same is true for warfare, and cites the Eskimos as evidence for this.

The Eskimos are a nomadic people who have no concept of war, even though they cannot be described as pacifists. Mead described how fights, theft of wives (!), murder and cannibalism were a part of Eskimo life. What was not part of Eskimo life was the organisation of one group of people to maim and kill another group of people. It might be possible to argue that Eskimos do not have war because they are nomadic and because they have few possessions. (It also might be because they are so chuffing cold.) However, to challenge this, Mead presented examples of other nomadic groups with few possessions who have developed all the rituals of warfare.

Mead's account is a little more optimistic than the others in this section because it suggests we are not the victims of our nature. She does, however, point out that once people have invented something they rarely go back and stop using it. The way forward, she suggests, is to invent a better way of dealing with conflict than warfare. She observed the development of justice in Western society over the last few hundred years from trial by ordeal through to trial by jury. People invented new ways of dealing with justice when the old way no longer worked and a better way was available. She suggested the same might be possible for the elimination of warfare.

Summary

The above historical contributions on the nature of human warfare present a largely pessimistic view of the future. The general picture appears to be that war is likely to continue because we have natural tendencies to be aggressive or we have, at least, learnt how effective warfare can be. The theories produce few, if any, testable hypotheses and they depend on whether we are the victims of our biology or whether we are able to shape our own destiny through the development of better ways of living. I believe in the second view and I'm prepared to fight anyone who disagrees with me (weak ironic humour).

Imagine all the people...

Use the above information along with your skill and judgement to answer the following question. If we had a world without war, what difference would it make to

(a) everyday behaviour in a shopping centre
(b) international trade
(c) major sports events like the Olympics
(d) how we settle disputes between groups of people

How has psychology been used in warfare?

Psychology has been involved in many aspects of warfare throughout the twentieth century. In this section, I will try to give you a flavour of that involvement and relate it where possible to psychological concepts and studies from the mainstream of psychology.

Early work in military psychology

Up until the 1960s, military psychology was mainly concerned with the same issues that would concern any major employer of people:

* selection of appropriate staff;
* matching people (soldiers) to machines;
* training (military) specialists;
* staff welfare.

The selection of the right person for the right job is a concern of any employer, and none more so than the military. In fact, the first mass IQ testing was carried out on the soldiers of the US Army during the First World War (1914–18). This work is described by Gould (1981), who noted how the data from this mass testing was used to promote a range of unpleasant political ideas including racist immigration laws in the USA. The testing also marked the start of the extensive military use of psychometric testing for the selection of staff (for more details on this work see Chapter 5).

On the issue of matching soldiers to machines, it is very important that any machine should be as easy to use as possible and as free from error as possible. For those of you who drive more than one car, you might well have come across a vehicle with the indicator control on the opposite side to your usual vehicle. This means that you keep switching on the window wipers every time you want to turn right. This is not a big problem, but it would be a different story if pressing the wrong lever didn't turn the wipers on, but instead launched a thermo-nuclear attack on Bournemouth.

An illustration of this problem occurred during the Second World War (1939–45), and it came about because the military had concentrated on training pilots to fly aircraft rather than designing aircraft that could be flown by pilots. They discovered that even very experienced pilots were prone to make errors with the poorly designed control systems. For example, similar-looking controls operating the landing gear and the steering flaps on some B-25 bombers were placed next to each other. The unfortunate consequence of this was that several B-25s were brought into land without the landing gear in place and so landed on their bellies. The pilots believed that they had activated the landing gear, but in fact they had just steered the plane (Mark *et al.*, 1987). Observations like this led to the development of aircraft controls that more nearly matched the capabilities of pilots.

The issue of staff welfare is also one that concerns large employers, if only for the reason that they do not want their staff being off work with sickness. One of the early attempts at health education at work can be dated to the work of Lashley and Watson during the First World War (1914–18) in their attempt to reduce the incidence of sexually transmitted disease in the American troops. Lashley and Watson (1921) investigated the impact of two films about venereal disease and surveyed and interviewed over one thousand people who saw the films. They found that 70 per cent had a good knowledge of the points made in the film, though, sadly, they found no evidence that the films had any effect on behaviour either to avoid sex with prostitutes or to take health precautions.

It is an interesting footnote that Lashley and Watson made a number of observations that are relevant today, and remarkably do not seem to have been addressed throughout the eighty years since they were made. Baggaley (1991) reviewed the media campaigns on HIV/AIDS and concluded that they did not take the lessons first observed by Lashley and Watson. Baggaley concluded that the various mass media campaigns often contained the following features: (a) the use of storylines, (b) the attempt to create a great sense of fear, and (c) the use of amusing or dramatic styles to get the message across. These common features of the HIV/AIDS campaign were the same as the features that were identified by Lashley and Watson as having a negative effect in a health education campaign during the First World War (1914–18).

Animals at war

Another area where psychology was able to contribute to military action was in training animals to take part in combat. Most famous among these attempts was the work of Skinner (1960) during the Second World War (1939–45) to train pigeons to navigate missiles to enemy targets. With startling originality, but admirable direct-ness, the programme was called 'Project Pigeon'. This was not the first time, nor the last, that the potential of animals was exploited in warfare. Skinner reported that the British Navy used sea gulls to detect submarines in the First World War (1914–18). The Navy sent its own submarines into the English Channel to release food. This attracted flocks of sea gulls who learnt to associate the sight of an underwater vessel with the appearance of food. They would then follow any submarine whether it was British or German. Therefore, a flock of seagulls in the Channel would be the sign of an approaching German submarine. Dogs and dolphins are among the other animals that have been used for military purposes, and the consequences for these animals was often not a good meal, but an early death as the explosives which were attached to them were detonated.

To cut a long, though interesting, story short, Skinner showed that his pigeons could accurately pilot a missile to seek out ships, and could then discriminate between different types of ships so that they could fly past allied ships and dive on to enemy ships. The military got as far as modifying some of their missiles to accommodate the pigeons and their tracking apparatus. However, the pigeons were never brought into active service, most likely because the military were uneasy at the thought of heavily armed pigeons flying overhead. Those of you who have ever stood in Trafalgar Square will immediately see the problem.

Military psychology after the 1960s

An article in *American Psychologist* by Windle and Vallance (1964) reflected the change that was beginning to take place in military psychology in the 1960s. The article suggested that psychology was turning its attention to paramilitary issues, for example, studies to investigate the political motivations of guerrilla fighters, the human factors in underground organisations and so on. Some of the other issues that this new type of psychology investigated were:

* the effects of captivity
* interrogation techniques
* brain-washing

It is not possible to give a full account of what is going on in military psychology since, not surprisingly, only a part of it is ever made public. Watson (1980) carried out a thorough review of this work, and I recommend his book to you if you are interested to find out more. In his research he unearthed 7,500 studies around the world, sponsored by a range of organisations. He goes on to suggest that many studies do not see the light of day because they are classified as military secrets or have some other restriction put on the information. The following takes a very selective look at some of the issues raised by Watson and others.

The effects of captivity

Watson (1980) describes a study carried out on survivors from Japanese prisoner of war (POW) camps during the Second World War (1939–45). The study suggests that the Japanese were unprepared for large numbers of POWs, with the result that the guards were allowed to develop their own ways of dealing with the prisoners. The conditions in the camps were crowded and dirty and the food was in short supply. A number of tortures were used including beatings, standing to attention in the sun for hours, pulling out the hair or fingernails and keeping the POWs' eyelids open with sticks and forcing them to look at the sun for hours.

The prisoners avoided talk and thoughts of home because this was too painful. Instead they talked about the work they had to do, and food they might eat. Internal discipline declined and food was often stolen. Depression and anxiety were common initial responses though they were often replaced by a lack of emotional responses to the point where the prisoners were unable to laugh or cry. Another common effect of the captivity and hunger was a range of cognitive deficits including difficulty in concentration and loss of memory. Many soldiers remained in the camps for years until the end of the war, and many others did not survive the experience.

The general conclusions of this and many other studies are that reactions to captivity are affected by two main factors: the physical hardships of the confinement, and the unpredictable and cruel behaviour of the guards.

This brings us to a famous study in social psychology by Zimbardo (see Haney *et al.*, 1973) on the psychological effects of captivity. In this study a number of young, healthy males were kept in a mock prison in the basement of the Stanford University psychology department. The captivity produced such dramatic effects that the study had the be stopped after only six days to prevent further psychological harm to the participants. This study is often described in the context of civilian prisons, but it is possible to see it in a very different light. The study was funded by the US Navy, and many of the features of the experiment did not correspond to the experience of people taken to prison after breaking the law.

The differences from the civilian prison experience included:

- the surprise arrest of the subjects and the immediate imprisonment. This is more like the experience of a hostage or a POW rather than a criminal.
- the depersonalisation of the prisoners through clothing and changes in their appearance. Prisoners in Western jails are not depersonalised in this way.

- the freedom of the guards to develop their own procedures and to apply their own rules as they liked. Again, this is more the experience of the hostage or POW than the criminal.
- the prisoners were referred to by their number only, whereas in Western jails they are referred to by name as well as number. POWs, on the other hand, are often referred to by number alone.

It seems unlikely that the US Navy has any interest in the running of civilian prisons. It does, however, have an interest in preparing its personnel to deal with captivity and cope with the inevitable stress of such an experience. Perhaps this interest was the underlying reason for the Zimbardo study.

Interrogation techniques

Prisoners are interrogated most commonly when someone believes they have information of value to the captors. The prisoners might well be under instruction to disclose nothing, and therefore the captor might employ a range of techniques to encourage disclosure. In many armies it is a military offence to collaborate with the enemy, and soldiers who talk too readily are prosecuted when they return home. Many of the interrogation techniques involve pain or discomfort, though they have only a limited effect. A lot of interest has centred on ways of making people more talkative using psychological techniques.

One of the most prominent of these techniques is **sensory deprivation**. This involves reducing the amount of perceptual stimulation that a person has to a minimum. This might involve solitary confinement in a warm room with low or no light and little or no sound. Some people find this very stressful, and most people find that it creates some sensory distortions. Watson (1980) refers to the extensive work carried out in this field for the American and Canadian military. He reports how, under sensory deprivation conditions, people often experienced hallucinations, an inability to distinguish between sleep and wakefulness and a distortion in their sense of time. Moreover, when they were released from the sensory deprivation they often felt overwhelmed by the colours and noises of everyday life, felt light-headed and were rather talkative (key point this). The sensory deprivation studies included investigations on the effects of the experience on conformity to group pressure (this depended on intelligence, with lower IQ scorers becoming more conformist and higher IQ scorers becoming less conformist) and response to propaganda (no obvious effect).

A variation on the sensory deprivation technique was used by the British Army in Northern Ireland in the early days of the Troubles. Shallice (1973) reported on twelve internees who were subjected to a horrifying interrogation technique. In the gaps between direct interrogation, the men were hooded in a black woven bag, subjected to very loud white noise and forced to stand against a wall with their hands above their heads. They were required to stand there for up to sixteen hours, and if they moved they were beaten. The internees were required to wear loose boiler suits, were deprived of sleep and put on a restricted diet. This treatment had a devastating effect on the men, who had major physical, cognitive and emotional responses.

It might well be that this material makes you feel very uneasy, and to be honest, that is also the response I get. It would be surprising, however, if a book about controversial issues in psychology did not have some bits that are disturbing. It is important to recognise that not all psychology is about amusing issues like body language or dating, and that it can have applications that some of us would want to challenge.

In summary, it would appear from the range of studies carried out that disorientation of prisoners is effective in increasing their willingness to talk. This disorientation can be achieved through, among other means, unpredictable torture, sleep deprivation, drugs, hunger and sensory deprivation.

Brain-washing

Is it possible to change someone's personality and behaviour to the extent where they seem to be a different person with a different set of attitudes and beliefs? The jury still appears to be out on this point, but the alarm about the techniques of brain-washing or re-education has been around since the Korean War in the 1950s. During this war, around 7,000 Americans were captured while serving overseas in Korea, and about one-third of these prisoners collaborated with the Koreans either by giving information or by making propaganda statements on behalf of the Koreans.

The conditions of captivity in Korea were harsh and the prisoners spent much of their time in indoctrination sessions. They were subjected to brutal treatment and allowed little contact with the outside world. Many American prisoners died in captivity, though it is interesting to note that Turkish prisoners kept under the same conditions survived to a man. The survivors were studied at some length to discover what happened, and also to develop ways of resisting this sort of treatment.

Dr Vincent

A harrowing first-hand account of Chinese re-education was given by a French doctor who had been working in China for twenty years (Lifton, 1961). He had a successful practice and his patients included several officials of the Chinese Communist Party. He was totally unprepared, then, for the day when five men arrested him at gunpoint and took him to a 're-education centre', where he spent the next three and a half years.

Lifton reported that the most intense experience of the re-education took place during the first three months of his imprisonment. Dr Vincent was kept in a small cell with eight Chinese prisoners, who were all very advanced in personal reform and eager to reform others for merits towards their own release. He had to sit in the middle of the cell and was addressed only by his prison number. All the other prisoners gathered around him and denounced him as a 'spy' and an 'imperialist'. He was told to recognise his crimes and confess. Any protestations of innocence were met with the response that the government had proof and would not have arrested him for nothing. This struggle, as it was called, continued for several hours at a time and was repeated often during the first period of his imprisonment.

Sometimes Dr Vincent was taken out for interrogation by three people and asked to confess. When he refused he was dragged back to the cell for more struggle with his fellow prisoners. Eventually, the effects of continual struggle and sleep deprivation took their toll and he made extravagant confessions about his involvement with espionage. These claims were not true and so he was unable to substantiate them under close interrogation. The interrogation continued without sleep and always in chains. Eventually at the point of exhaustion he started to confess to what his captors wanted, denouncing his friends and associates and he started to see things from 'the people's standpoint'.

After eight weeks in detention the chains were finally removed and he was allowed to sit down during interrogation. He was now offered friendly guidance in rewriting his confession over and over again. He was also introduced to the cell routine which had strict control over the prisoners, for example, allowing them two dashes to the toilet per day when they had to run to the toilet and were allowed only forty-five seconds to complete their activities.

For the next three years, Dr Vincent took part in the study programme in his cell, learning to understand the world from the point of view of his captors. His fellow prisoners were called 'school-mates' and his captors were called 'instructors'. Discussion would take place for twelve hours every day. In the third year of his captivity he began to live in harmony with his captors and began looking forward to a sentence for his crimes, maybe twenty-five years' hard labour. Eventually, he read out his confession in front of the television cameras and publicly signed it. He was taken to court and allowed to leave China.

Once free, he found adjustment back into Western life quite difficult and commented, 'It's not that I miss it [the prison], but I find it was more easy.' Dr Vincent came to believe that he had been seriously wronged by the Chinese authorities but he experienced a change in himself that made him more willing to open himself to others and more sensitive to other people's inner feelings.

If we identify the key sequence of events for Dr Vincent, we can see the general pattern of the brainwashing process:

- arrest;   complete and unexpected removal from his daily life;
- depersonalisation;   through, for example, being referred to by number;
- struggle;   through argument to see things from his captors point of view;
- leniency;   small indulgences and signs of human contact and acceptance;
- loss of control;   of all aspects of his life such as toilet functions;
- study;   self analysis for hours on end every day;
- change;   finally see the world from another viewpoint.

Of course, if you believe that this process helped Dr Vincent to see the correct viewpoint on life, then you would see this process as education rather than indoctrination. This is the moral problem at the heart of any attempt to change attitudes and behaviour, and we will come back to that in Chapter 2 on propaganda.

Summary

The above gives a flavour of some of issues in the application of psychology to warfare. There are numerous other issues that have been investigated, including how soldiers behave in groups, what makes a good military leader, what are the effects of being under fire, and why some soldiers commit atrocities. All of these issues, and many more, have attracted a lot of interest from various military organisations, and as long as wars continue in different parts of the world they will have loads of material for their research and many applications for the findings of that research. Of course, one of the most prominent of all psychological activities in warfare and the control of people is the use of propaganda, and we will look at that in the next section. Before that, we will have a brief look at the some of the effects of war.

What can psychology tell us about the effects of war?

One of the clearest summaries of the effects of war is contained in the report on nuclear war written by the British Psychological Society (Thompson, 1985). The report was written to review the best psychological evidence available on all aspects of nuclear war. It appears a little dated now because there no longer seems to be a threat of full-scale nuclear war between two large and heavily armed countries, but it does still have much to say about the consequences of war. It considered responses to previous wars and natural disasters so as to build up a picture of how people would deal with large-scale destruction and mass civilian casualties. The report can be used in the planning of civil defence so that we can be better prepared to deal with disastrous events.

One of the effects of war that has started to attract more attention in recent years has been the long-term psychological consequences on people who lived through warfare. A focus for this work is the condition known as **post-traumatic stress disorder**. The concept of this condition grew out of work in many different fields of traumatic stress, for example the condition referred to as 'shell-shock' during the First World War. It took a long time, however, for the condition to be actually recognised as a syndrome in its own right, and for the military, as well as others, to realise that it was actually a psychiatric disorder resulting from traumatic experiences, and not just cowardliness or an over-vivid imagination.

Post-traumatic stress disorder was first described in the third edition of the *Diagnostic and Statistical Manual of the American Psychiatric Association* (DSM-III) in 1980. The condition has three main groups of symptoms: re-experiencing phenomena (for example recurrent and intrusive distressing memories of the traumatic event or situation), avoidance or numbing reactions (such as efforts to avoid the thoughts or feelings associated with the trauma, and feeling of being detached or estranged from other people) and symptoms of increased arousal (such as difficulty in staying asleep, irritability and outbursts of anger).

These are not qualitatively different from the experiences which a non-sufferer will have after a traumatic event, and everyone has some reaction to a disaster or tragedy. What distinguishes the individual with post-traumatic stress disorder is the breadth, severity and endurance of the symptoms. The condition is cyclical, and the symptoms can disappear and reappear. They can also appear some time after the event, even several months or years, and the delayed versions of the condition are no less severe.

Not everyone reacts in the same way to traumatic events, and it is relatively unpredictable who will develop post-traumatic stress disorder and who will make a speedy re-adjustment. However, if the stress is serious enough, and prolonged, there is some suggestion that everyone will succumb in time. Swank (1949) studied 4,000 survivors of the Normandy campaign (in the Second World War, 1939–45), and found that all soldiers became incapacitated after three-quarters of their companions had been killed. Moreover, Archibald *et al.* (1963) found that even as late as fifteen years after a traumatic event, 70 per cent of survivors showed symptoms of PTSD.

Recent studies have shown that the effects of trauma can be life-long. In a study of over 700 veterans of the Second World War (1939–45), Hunt (1997) found that around 20 per cent appeared to have post-traumatic stress according to one of the psychometric scales used to measure this condition (the Impact of Events Scale). Hunt reported that many of the veterans still experienced intrusive thoughts about the war, often in the form of war-related dreams. Bear in mind that over fifty years have passed since the end of this war. Some had coped with the experience by avoiding any reminders. For example one of the veterans said:

> I never told anybody anything, the wife and daughter knew nothing about being a POW.
>
> (Hunt 1997, p. 359)

The condition of post-traumatic stress is not confined to combatants. Waugh (1997) looked at the impact of the Second World War on women civilians. Many of these experienced war at first hand, especially if they lived in the major cities that experienced heavy bombing. Some of these women showed the same type of intrusive thoughts and avoidance found in combatants with post-traumatic stress.

Summary

We are becoming increasingly aware of how war can have damaging psychological effects on civilians as well as the combatants. One of the controversies that this work provokes is whether we should try to help people with stress reactions so that they can deal more effectively with war (and therefore maybe prolong it), or whether psychology should encourage people to deal with the stress by opposing war and so reducing the opportunities for the stress occurring in future generations.

Imagine you are interrogating a family member to find out where they have hidden your collection of football stickers/nail polish.

- Identify three techniques to encourage them to talk.
- Estimate how long it will take to make them crack.
- Consider what they can do to resist you.
- Don't you think you are having too much fun thinking about this?

Review exercise

Further reading

Taylor, A.J.P. (1963) *The First World War: An Illustrated History*, Harmondsworth: Penguin. Any book on one of the great military campaigns would give some insight into how war is conducted. This one contains a number of photographs showing the horror of the 1914–18 war.

Watson, P. (1980) *War on the Mind: The Military Uses and Abuses of Psychology*, London: Penguin. This is a comprehensive account of the uses of psychology in warfare with numerous examples from a range of military organisations.

2

Psychology and propaganda

Introduction

What is propaganda? There is no easy answer, to this since it depends on what attitudes you hold to start with. If you agree with a political message you might view it as a statement of fact, but if you do not agree with it you might see it as manipulative propaganda. The following sections explore some of the key features of persuasive messages and propaganda using examples from three military conflicts of the twentieth century. We will then go on to look at some of the techniques used by politicians in their attempt to get us to agree with them. We will start by looking at what we mean by propaganda and persuasive messages.

The word propaganda is derived from the Latin word *propagare*, which refers to a gardener's practice of pinning fresh shoots of a plant into the earth so that they grow and become separate plants. So, if we take it literally, propaganda means 'that which is to be spread'. The term was first used in its modern sense by the Catholic church during the seventeenth century to describe the spread of Christianity. This was thought to be a good thing if you were a Catholic (but a bad thing if you were not a Catholic), and the people conducting the propaganda did not see their work as devious or underhand. Today, though, the term has some very sinister connotations.

There is an overlap between propaganda and education. Both activities try to inform people and change people, but one we see as a generally good thing, and the other we deny having anything to do with. McGuire (1973) makes a number of distinctions between education and propaganda (see Table 2.1), though it is fair to say that many messages fall between the two sets of criteria.

When we think of propaganda one of the first images that comes to mind is that of posters designed to help 'the war effort', or in other words to encourage people to accept the war that is taking place,

Table 2.1 Distinctions between education and propaganda

	Education	Propaganda
Aims		
1	change attitudes	change feelings
2	change factual and verifiable beliefs	change beliefs about matters of taste or unverifiable issues
Motives		
3	the source of the message is disinterested and does not stand to gain from the acceptance of the message	the source is prejudiced and stands to profit from the success of the communication
4	the source does not intend to deceive	the source intends to deceive
Content		
5	correct information and rational argument	incorrect or selective information and emotional argument
Effect		
6	impact comes about through the receiver's attention and comprehension	impact is determined by the receiver yielding
7	retention	action

Source: McGuire (1973)

Figure 2.1 **Example of an 'atrocity story' propaganda message**

accept the sacrifices they are making and to work harder. An example from the Second World War is shown in Figure 2.1. One of the common themes of British propaganda at this time was the atrocity stories about the behaviour of the enemy. The aim of these images was to encourage people to continue the fight by suggesting (a) we must not let these bad people win, and (b) we are the good guys and we are fighting for a good cause (it is a just war). Rumours circulated about the Germans, for example, that they boiled the corpses of enemy soldiers to make soap. Some of the atrocity stories had a small amount of truth, though others were entirely made up (Pratkanis and Aronson, 1992).

Propaganda was a major concern of social scientists during the 1960s and 1970s. Propaganda was seen as being carried out by THEM – the bad guys (who were usually the Communist countries of China and the Soviet Union and their allies) and education was conducted by US – the good guys (Europe and the USA and their allies). It was believed that propaganda could have a dramatic effect on people and encourage them to believe in extreme political philosophies and carry out morally indefensible behaviour. The most powerful means of propaganda was thought to be delivered through large rallies, stirring speeches, controlled television messages and a structured curriculum in schools. It is no longer appropriate to think about propaganda in this way for two reasons. First, there is little evidence that it ever had much effect (McGuire, 1985), and second, we receive information in different ways today, particularly through television and radio, which are very difficult for any government to control.

Persuasive messages

As we have already seen, it is difficult to consistently distinguish between propaganda and education, and this is one of the reasons that social psychology tends to consider this within the wider issue of persuasive messages. Many of the activities that used to be called propaganda are now called 'news management'. The change of the term is a piece of propaganda in itself. By using a neutral term like 'news management' rather than the slightly sinister term 'propaganda', the activity takes on a different light to the point where politicians, business people and the military might boast about their news management successes. News management is a more subtle process than propaganda, but the two share a lot of features in common and we can put them both under the heading of persuasive messages. In Chapter 3 of this text we will look at another example of persuasive messages when we consider advertising. In this chapter, though we will first look at some of the psychological research that provides a framework for considering persuasive messages.

The Yale research on persuasive communication

The early work on persuasive messages was carried out by Carl Hovland (for example, 1953) and his associates at Yale University.

Hovland took the approach of **learning theory** and believed that a message will change a person's attitude or behaviour if the person believes they will obtain some reinforcement from the change. That reinforcement could, for example, be the approval of important people, or it could be financial.

The Yale group identified some key stages in this process of change:

1   *Exposure*: the target of the message must see or hear it for the message to have any influence. Although this sounds incredibly obvious, it is difficult to ensure that target groups actually receive messages.
2   *Attention*: once they are exposed to the message, the target must pay attention to it, and with many political messages this is difficult because as soon as the words 'This is a party political broadcast on behalf of...' are spoken, the channel has already been changed.
3   *Comprehension*: the target does not need to understand everything that is said in the message, but they must understand the conclusion if it is going to influence them.
4   *Acceptance*: once they have understood the message, they have to accept it if change is to take place.
5   *Retention*: the target does not need to remember the message, but they do need to hang on to the new attitude.
6   *Change in behaviour*: the new attitude has to be one that guides behaviour if the desired result of behavioural change is to be achieved.

Research on the Yale approach

A lot of research was carried out on the effect of messages on attitudes and behaviour, though it is beyond the scope of this text to review it in full (some more details of this approach are covered in Chapter 3, on advertising). Two examples of the work will give a flavour of it: the sleeper effect, and the selective attention we apply to political messages.

The **sleeper effect** was first described by Hovland *et al.* (1949), who noticed that the source of the message had a big effect on how it was received. If the source of the message was respected then the message had a much greater initial impact than if the source was not respected.

For example, a message from a respected politician will have a bigger effect than a message from a drunk man in a public bar. This effect diminished over time, however, and the effect of the respected source declined while the effect of the unrespected source increased. It appeared that people remembered the message and forgot the source. So, if you sleep on it, the message will have a different effect on you and the influence of the source will diminish. Subsequent research challenged this finding, and it appears that the sleeper effect only occurs under certain conditions. Pratkanis *et al.* (1988) found that the sleeper effect will occur if (a) the message is more memorable than the source, and (b) the message would have been persuasive in the first place if it were not for the unrespected source.

On the issue of attention to messages, it is now an established finding that we tune in to messages we want to hear and messages with which we agree, and tune out of messages with which we disagree. As early as 1960, during the first televised presidential debates in the US elections, it was observed that viewers would pay attention when their preferred candidate was speaking (either Kennedy or Nixon) but would look away or do something else when the other candidate was speaking (Sigel, 1964). The Yale research produced many findings that are used today by, for example, politicians, advertisers and health educators.

Intuitive psychology

Social psychology records and investigates human behaviour. Some people have an intuitive grasp of that behaviour without the need for research. In the field of persuasion some people have shown great skill over the centuries in their ability to affect others. Adolf Hitler is demonised as one of the most manipulative propagandists of the twentieth century, and if you read the quote from him below and compare it to the Yale list of key stages above, you will see he had a grasp of the principles of persuasion without ever studying psychology.

> The receptive ability of the masses is very limited, their under-standing small; on the other hand, they have a great power of forgetting. This being so, all propaganda must be confined to a very few points which must be brought out in the form of

slogans until the very last man is enabled to comprehend what is meant by any slogan. If this principle is sacrificed by the desire to be many-sided, it will dissipate the effectual working of the propaganda, for the people will be unable to digest or retain the material that is offered to them.

(Hitler, 1925, p. 77)

Along with this analysis of propaganda messages, Hitler also introduced the mass political rally. These rallies, most famously at Nuremberg, involved an audience of thousands who played their own part in the emotionally charged events. The rallies were carefully planned theatrical events where the music and settings and speakers were all choreographed to produce the most dramatic effect. The audience were wound up for an hour or more with singing and chanting before the speeches began, and this gave the speeches even more emotional charge. We do not have any research findings on the effect of these rallies on the people who were there or the people who saw them on film in the cinema, though it seems likely they did much to give people a sense of belonging to a strong and popular movement.

Look back at the distinction between propaganda and education, and consider which term best describes the following:

- your psychology lessons
- health campaigns designed to discourage smoking
- party political election broadcasts
- advertisements from British Nuclear Fuels encouraging you to visit their reprocessing plant at Sellafield
- television news

Progress exercise

Examples of propaganda campaigns

Allied propaganda to German soldiers during the Second World War (1939–45)

Shils and Janowitz (1948) reviewed the effectiveness of Allied propaganda on German troops towards the end of the war when the Germans were losing. It is, perhaps, at this time in any conflict that propaganda will have the greatest effect since morale is likely to be declining and the fear of the final outcome must be rising. The aim of this propaganda was to lower the morale of the German troops and to encourage them to surrender. During the last three years of the war, a large number of leaflets and newsletters were dropped behind enemy lines, and their readership and effect was measured through interviews of German soldiers who subsequently surrendered or were captured.

The interviews suggested that the leaflets did not have a very great effect. The German POWs had often read the leaflets and often reported believing them, but they did not seem to affect behaviour in the battlefield. In Normandy (on the north coast of France) for example, it was estimated during one campaign that over 90 per cent of the German troops read the Allied leaflets, but this period of fighting was particularly noteworthy for the high level of German morale and the stiff resistance they offered to Allied advances.

In general, it was estimated that Allied leaflets were seen by between 60–80 per cent of German troops, who also circulated them amongst their comrades. The Allied Psychological Warfare Division published a daily news-sheet (*Nachrichten für die Truppe*) which was dropped behind enemy lines, and it was estimated that each copy that was picked up had a readership of between four and five soldiers.

Tactical and strategic propaganda

Shils and Janowitz made a distinction between tactical propaganda and strategic propaganda. Tactical propaganda tries to get an immediate effect in a tactical situation. This was commonly achieved through loudspeaker appeals to the enemy which told them how they could surrender safely. This technique brought a lot of success: for example, the US Fourth Armoured Division reported that its psychological warfare unit captured over 500 prisoners during a four-day advance. The successful targets for this technique were often isolated units, or groups where their ability to function effectively had been destroyed.

Strategic propaganda, on the other hand, looked for a longer term effect. These leaflets concentrated on four main themes:

- ideological attacks on the Nazi Party and its war aims;
- the hopelessness of the German position;
- the justness of the Allied war aims;
- promises of good treatment for prisoners.

There was little evidence that the first point had any effect. The Allies conducted a monthly Psychological Warfare opinion poll of German POWs, and found no decline in support for the Nazis until the very last months of the war. The obvious major success of these campaigns was the leaflet that had a 'safe conduct pass'. It was written in an official style and contained the signature of the American commander-in-chief (General Eisenhower). It seems that the promise of good treatment as a POW was the most effective message.

Shils and Janowitz concluded by suggesting that the Allies began the war with high expectations of propaganda which were only partly fulfilled. During times when group solidarity was high among the German troops, it appears that the propaganda had little obvious effect, but when a group came under intense pressure brought about by military defeat, propaganda helped undermine German morale and facilitate the surrender of the troops.

American propaganda campaigns in Southeast Asia

It is hard to say when the Vietnam War started. In 1945 Ho Chi Minh proclaimed the Democratic Republic of Vietnam and initiated the final struggle to rid his country of its French colonial rulers. Interestingly, he looked to the USA as a friend of this new republic and used the words of the Declaration of Independence of the United States of America in his speech. The French were finally driven out ten years later, but not before the USA had started to become involved against the democratic aspirations of the Vietnamese people. This involvement was gradually increased and a military government that was favourable to the USA was established in the south of the country. For a ten-year period in the mid-1960s and 1970s the USA waged full-scale war against the Vietnamese people. To this day, it is not clear why they did it. The war ended in 1975 when the Americans were finally driven out of the country by the peasant army of the Vietnamese. At least 1,300,000 people were killed in the conflict and many thousands more were maimed. Of the dead, 58,022 were Americans (less than 5 per cent), the rest were Vietnamese (Pilger, 1989). It is one of the triumphs of Western propaganda that this war is seen today as America's tragedy. Our view of this conflict is seen through the eyes of the Americans and we rarely hear the voice of the Vietnamese people telling us how a poorly armed, rural people managed to endure mass destruction and mass murder, and go on to defeat the greatest fighting force on the planet.

The Americans had a different propaganda problem in Vietnam to the one in the Second World War described above by Shils and Janowitz. They could not target their efforts at the Vietnamese troops since they could never find them, so leaflet drops were carried out on a grand scale. They also directed their attention to the civilian population so that the latter would stop supporting the Vietnamese fighters. The Vietnamese fighters also used propaganda techniques, though they did not have the same level of resources at their disposal.

A review of US propaganda campaigns during the Vietnam War by Watson (1980) suggests that great efforts were made to encourage defection by the Vietnamese fighters. He quotes from military papers which estimate that during the month of March in 1969 the Americans dropped 713 million leaflets, and distributed a further three million by hand, all trying to encourage defection. During the same month 156,000 posters were distributed and 2,000 hours of broadcasting were used for the same purpose. The military report does not estimate the effectiveness of this campaign, but does note that the best way to encourage defection was through the stories of fighters who had already defected.

A first-hand account of psychological warfare activities during this period was given by the journalist John Pilger, who made several trips to Vietnam. The following is one of his diary entries.

Over Fire Base 'Snuffy', Tay Ninh province, South Vietnam, August 30, 1970. 'You could say the helicopter has been our salvation in this war,' says Captain Frank Littlewood, from Cleveland Ohio. 'Why, you could say that without the helicopter we wouldn't be doing so damm well in this war!' Captain Littlewood is a Psy-Ops officer of the U.S. First Air Cavalry Division whose colours include the crossed swords of Colonel Custer's Seventh Cavalry. Psy-Ops means Psychological Warfare.

'What we're doing today,' shouts Captain Littlewood over the noise of the rotors, 'is psyching out the enemy. We're going to play a tape we call Wandering Soul. Now you've got to understand the Vietnamese way of life to realise the power behind Wandering Soul. You see, the Vietnamese people worship their ancestors and they take a lot of notice of the spirits and stuff like that. Well, what we're going to do is fly low over the jungle and broadcast the voices of ancestors – you know, ghosts – which we've simulated in our studios. Got it? These ghosts – these ancestors, I mean – are going to tell the Vietcong to stop messing with people's rights to live freely, or they're going to disown them.'

Our helicopter drops to a few hundred feet above the trees. Captain Littlewood throws a switch and a reverberating voice emits from two loudspeakers. While the voice reverberates and occasionally hoots, a sergeant hurls out handfuls of leaflets which also offer ancestral threats. Captain Littlewood himself hurls out one unopened box of leaflets. 'Maybe,' he says, 'I'll hit one of them on the head and we won't have to worry about changing his mind.'

(Pilger, 1975, pp. 70–1)

Pilger also describes a number of other missions by Psy-Ops forces including one to encourage villagers to support the Americans by giving them toothbrushes and a chemical toilet. The aim of these missions was to win the hearts and minds of the civilian population, though it has to be said that at the start of these missions the village would be surrounded by heavily armed troops and then fortified with barbed wire. This probably acted as an encouragement for the Vietnamese people to brush their teeth vigorously.

Watson (1980) suggests that the above programmes were typical of Psy-Op propaganda tactics. He quotes military documents that show a social profile drawn up on a range of countries. These profiles included such information as

- prestigious people
- common gifts used by people to get to know each other
- waste and disposal patterns
- attitudes to leaders
- the opinions of these leaders

They also collected information on social and religious customs including such items as what smells each culture found most offensive. The propaganda tactic was then to target particular attitudes, prominent people and customs and beliefs. One example of this approach was the 'wandering souls' campaign witnessed by Pilger; another one concerned the grieving practices of the Vietnamese. It was the Vietnamese custom to remember deaths after 49 days and after 100 days, as well as on anniversaries. Leaflets were dropped by the Americans on these dates after big battles in areas where people would have been likely to have lost relatives. The aim was to increase the misery of those days and further undermine the morale of the Vietnamese.

The above two examples are among the more understandable of the propaganda campaigns. There were others that were less easy to comprehend. For example, during the Korean war the Americans collected information on graffiti in North Korean (their enemy) toilets. The study found very little political graffiti, but it did find occasions where the toilet paper was newspaper with a picture of the Korean Leader (Kim Il-Sung). The use of his picture in this way was strictly forbidden. It was decided to encourage this use by preparing toilet paper with the picture of Kim Il-Sung on the sheets to encourage...I'm not sure what. A further remarkable example was contained in a report by Howard and Hitt (described in Watson, 1980) of their anthropological research into smell. The aim of the research was to design stink bombs that would get to a specific culture. Different cultural groups have very different appreciation of smells, and Howard and Hitt looked for smells that would cause nausea or fright. These smells could be used to flush out guerrilla fighters into the open where they could be shot by American troops who, being from another culture, would not mind the smell at all. One example of their findings was that the Karen people of Burma and Northern Thailand were relatively unconcerned by many smells Western people find disgusting, but they feared the smell of cooking fat. So, if you are ever thinking of being lost in Burma, take a chip pan with you.

The Gulf War of 1991

The Gulf War was a very different conflict from the other two examples above. In the summer of 1990, Iraq invaded and annexed its neighbouring country of Kuwait. Under the political umbrella of the United Nations, a large armed forced led by the USA massed in Saudi Arabia and finally in 1991 attacked the Iraqi forces and forced them out of Kuwait. News management, in this case, was used specifically to keep the civilian populations of the attacking countries happy and in general agreement with the attack.

One of the themes of the comments made by British and American politicians was to associate Saddam Hussain (the leader of Iraq) with Adolf Hitler. One of the effects of associating two problems together is that it draws you to look for similar solutions to the problem. The general wisdom about the war with Germany and Hitler was that the Allies initially made the initial mistake of appeasing the German dictator when they should have opposed him. The lesson from history, therefore, is to oppose the dictators and not to appease them. Laboratory studies by Gilovich (1981) showed that when people were asked to make hypothetical decisions about a political crisis, one of the key variables that affected their decision was whether the information they were given made references to Nazi Germany or if it made references to the Vietnam conflict. The simple lesson that is often drawn from the Vietnam war is that America (or any other major power) should not get involved in a foreign conflict in which it has little primary interest. The people who were given material with links to Nazi Germany were more likely to favour military action than the people who were given material with links to the Vietnam war.

One of the ways of encouraging the British and American publics to accept military action against Iraq was to associate the conflict with the Second World War rather than Vietnam. The strategy appeared to work in the first instance, but it created problems for the Allies at the end of the conflict. The military campaign ended without taking over the whole of Iraq and without removing Saddam Hussain from power. It is not possible to imagine the end of the Second World War without the removal of Adolf Hitler and the Nazi government from power. The analogy broke down for the Gulf War as it became clear that the Allies did not see Saddam Hussain as Adolf Hitler. Pratkanis and Aronson (1992) suggested that this realisation marked the start of the decline in popularity of the American President, George Bush.

Managing the news

Even before the Gulf War started, a special unit in the US military took on the task of news management (Manheim, 1993). In particular, they were interested in the immunisation techniques first suggested by McGuire (1964). The aim of this approach was to prepare the population for some bad news and offer challenges to any likely negative messages.[1] The specific aims of the special unit were to:

- keep problems and foul-ups in perspective;
- preserve the credibility of the army;
- prevent surprises;
- create the 'right' first impressions and prevent 'false' impressions;
- keep everybody calm (Don't Panic!).

An example of this strategy was the way that they dealt with the threat of chemical warfare. The army was aware that Iraq had chemical weapons, and it also had evidence of their use in campaigns against the Kurds who were in conflict with the Iraqi government. These weapons were capable of inflicting very heavy casualties on the US forces, and rather than ignore the danger or play it down, the special unit initiated a series of briefings with reporters to get the subject on the agenda as early as possible. This strategy prepared people for potential bad news during the conflict.

---

1 A similar technique was used by the British Labour Party up to and during the General Election of 1997 with their 'rapid rebuttals unit'.

Controlling the media

The American government believed that it could only continue the conflict with Iraq while its own public supported the action. They believed that the negative press coverage of the Vietnam War had undermined the will of the American people to continue that war, and they wanted to avoid this happening again. The government needed to control the media reaction to this conflict, but they wanted to avoid excluding the press since this would affect the credibility of the operation. They obtained the result they wanted by flooding the area with journalists.

The military developed a 'Hometown News Program' which brought local journalists from all over the USA to the Gulf at the army's expense. In news conferences, the journalists all wanted to ask their own questions which were largely repetitive and relatively uninformed. This had the effect of squeezing out the more informed and critical national media. The military were also aware that in the USA the local media have more credibility than the national media, who are often seen as cynical. The Hometown News Program brought around 1,500 journalists to the Gulf during the conflict (Manheim, 1993) and helped manage the news output and keep it local and simple. This news management succeeded in keeping damaging items off the public agenda, including the idea that American soldiers were being asked to risk their lives for the sake of oil. This could have been very damaging for President Bush because of his connections with Texas oil companies and his personal links with Kuwait made through this oil connection (Wayne, 1993).

Another aspect of the news management by the American military was to avoid all estimates of Iraqi casualties. These were not released until after the conflict when a government worker followed her normal procedure and released this information to a reporter on request. She was removed from her job and her files disappeared from her desk. The estimates for Iraqi war deaths were 86,194 men, 39,612 women, and 32,195 children.

The news for public consumption had one final component and that was the demonisation of the Iraqis. The Kuwaitis employed a consultancy in the USA which spent over $11 million on putting their case across. This agency is reported to have been the source of the infamous story of Iraqi soldiers pulling new-born Kuwaiti children from their incubators so they could steal the equipment. A young woman gave evidence to the American Congress that she had witnessed this first hand. It was later discovered, however, that the young women was the daughter of the Kuwaiti Ambassador to the USA and she had been coached in her evidence by the consultancy (Manheim, 1993).

The persuasive techniques of politicians

Politicians use a wide range of techniques to encourage us to support them, and we will look at some examples in this section. One important skill is to encourage applause from an audience, and research on this was described by Eagle (1980). One of the techniques identified is the 'repetition and sign off' used at the end of a speech to tell people when to start clapping. The example given below comes from James Callaghan, who was Labour Prime Minister at the time when he made the speech:

> 'As long as there's a family without a home,
> as long as there's a patient waiting for a
> hospital bed,
> as long as there's a man or woman without a
> job
> or someone who suffers from discrimination
> because of their colour,
> so long will our work as a Labour govern-
> ment not be done.
> We go forward in that spirit and that resolve.'
> (Applause)
>
> (Eagle, 1980, p. 33)

Some political speakers can key in this applause so well that it starts before they have stopped speaking, and this makes it look even more spontaneous.

One technique that can gain applause during a speech is to use contrast. An example comes from a speech given by Labour Politician Tony Benn to a special conference of the party in 1980:

'We shall find two or three million demor-
alised long term unemployed
who have to be put back to work in factories
not that Hitler has *bombed*
but that Thatcher and Joseph have *closed*'
(Applause)

(Eagle 1980, p. 34)

If you listen to the speeches of politicians, especially at their party conferences, you will be able to hear these and other techniques. You might also notice another observation of the research, that mid-speech applause almost always lasts for eight seconds, which suggests that a political audience knows how to play its part in the unfolding drama of the speech.

Personalising the issue

One way of deflecting criticism of a government is to talk about indi-vidual people and look at the problems of one person rather than most people. In this way you can single out a person who has done well and so infer that all people are doing well or could do well. American President Ronald Reagan was often referred to as the 'Great Communicator', and one of his techniques was to personalise issues in this way. For example, when talking on the issue of poverty he referred to a Vietnamese refugee by name and described her rags-to-riches story since her arrival in the USA. He also talked about a Black woman who had started up a home for the children of drug-addicted mothers. These two stories showed how poverty was a personal issue that could be overcome and that social problems could be dealt with by personal initiative rather than government interven-tion (Pratkanis and Aronson, 1992). This type of speech can bring about an emotional response in the audience, but it ignores the many counter-examples of people who continue to struggle with poverty and poor conditions.

Granfalloon

The 'minimal group paradigm' is a term used to describe the work of Henri Tajfel (for example, 1970) which showed that people can easily be encouraged to support a group of strangers just by drawing attention to some supposed similarity between the individual and the strangers, for example, 'these people are all Capricorns just like you'. The term 'granfalloon' comes from American author Kurt Vonnegut, and is used in many texts to describe this effect. Granfalloons are proud and meaningless associations of human beings. The granfalloon has a cognitive and motivational effect. On the cognitive side, it helps categorise the world and make sense of it. On the motivational side, we derive self-esteem and pride from the groups we belong to, so we are likely to defend our own group and look down on opposing groups.

Politicians use the granfalloon technique to encourage people to feel part of a political or military enterprise and to feel hostile towards people in other groups. The extreme example of this is the use of racial groups as scapegoats. The propaganda used in Nazi Germany identified the Jews as a group of people responsible for the problems of the German people. It was designed to encourage German identity by identifying and demonising people who were not German. It is a technique that was not unique to Nazi Germany, and it is a common technique of politicians to make us feel part of group of which they are an important part.

Summary

Propaganda is often presented as a simple process that attempts to change people's behaviour by shouting loudly and using capital letters. Psychology's contribution has been to make this a much more sophisticated process, and a process that it is often hard to detect. The messages involve mild distortion of information through to the manufacture of persuasive stories. Propaganda also involves cultural analysis that allows the propagandist to target key issues in people's lives and attempt to change their attitudes and behaviour. Today, when we listen to news messages and promotional messages for products, we know that every message has the hand of news management on it. The question is, whose hand is on this bit of news?

Review what you have learnt in this chapter by designing a simple propaganda campaign to encourage people to vote for the Monster Raving Loony Party at the next election. Your should consider

- the message
- how you will present it
- who you will present it to
- what medium you will use

Further reading

Pilger, J. (1989) *Heroes*, London: Pan. John Pilger gives his very personal and direct accounts of his experiences as a journalist in some of the major war zones of the last thirty years.

Pratkanis, A.R. and Aronson, E. (1992) *Age of Propaganda: The Everyday Use and Abuse of Persuasion*, New York: W.H. Freeman. Engagingly written with a wide range of examples.

Psychology and advertising

Introduction

Promotional messages are part of our daily experience. The slogans and jingles are only just below the surface of our consciousness. It's the taste of a new generation. The car in front is … going faster than you. But hey, eight out of ten owners said their cats preferred it, and, anyway, it's the real thing, so just do it! Advertising phrases might be part of our everyday speech, but do advertisements really work, and what types of psychology do advertisers use to get us to buy their overpriced Tee-shirts with a little squiggle on the neck band?

One of the aims of advertising is to make us change our behaviour. It attempts to do this by changing our feelings, changing our attitudes or by encouraging us to copy behavioural models. In the first part of this chapter we will look at some psychological approaches to attitude change. We will then go on to look at how psychology has been applied to the way we purchase products, and finally we will have a brief look at the psychology of products.

The psychology of attitudes and attitude change

The study of attitude change has attracted the attention of many psychologists who have published a vast amount of research. According to Lindzey and Aronson (1985), over 1,000 new research articles are published each year on this topic. Part of the interest centres around the effects of the mass media on our attitudes. One of the major changes in social behaviour during the twentieth century was due to the growth of mass communications. It is estimated that people in Europe and the USA spend, on average, between three and four hours each day receiving communication from the mass media, which is about twice as much time as they spend socialising (McGuire, 1985). In this section we will look at the Yale model of communication (also see Chapter 2), and have a brief look at factoids.

The Yale model of communication

Although the research continues to develop, much of it is still concerned with the questions first developed by Hovland and his associates (for example, 1953). This is commonly referred to as the Yale model of communication (see also Chapter 2 on propaganda). This model identifies five key features to consider in the study of persuasive messages and their affect on attitudes (see Figure 3.1):

- the SOURCE of the message
- the features of the MESSAGE
- the MEDIUM used to put over the message
- the TARGET of the message
- the SITUATION that the message is received in

Source

The characteristics of the person who gives you the message (the source) will have an effect on the way you respond to it. Two of the factors that affect your responses are the credibility of the source and the attractiveness of the source. The general finding in advertising is that attractive sources have the greatest effect, or at least that is the

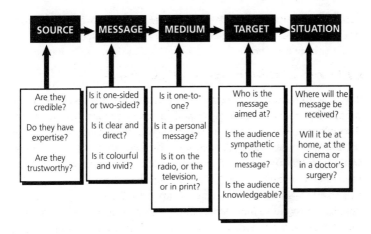

Figure 3.1 **The Yale model of communication**

belief of advertisers because they select attractive people to promote most products. It does not always work like that, however, as shown by Petty *et al.* (1983). They conducted a laboratory study on the effectiveness of messages for disposable razors when the messages were given by different sources. They used either well-liked sports celebrities or middle-aged local people. They also varied the quality of the message (either thoughtful arguments about the quality of the product, or meaningless statements about style and look), and the motivation of the viewers (offering some of them the reward of choosing a razor as a prize at the end of the study). The viewers who were offered a reward had an incentive to find out about the product because they were going to choose one later. These people were most affected by the quality of the message rather than the source. On the other hand, the viewers who had not been offered a reward and so were not going to need the information in the near future were more affected by the source, and favoured the advertisements with the sports celebrities. This suggests that the attractiveness of the source has less effect if the message is important to us.

We are more likely to respond to messages from a source who we think is like us. A study by Qualls and Moore (1990) asked over 100

Black people and over 100 White people to watch an advertisement for a new beer. They were asked to rate the advertisement, the actor and the beer, and then to taste the beer and evaluate it. The advertisements were varied in terms of the race and social class of the people portrayed, and the viewers also varied along the same dimensions. Qualls and Moore found that, with regard to race, people tended to prefer those advertisements portraying the same racial group: White viewers saw White actors more positively than Black actors, and Black viewers saw Black actors more positively than White ones. This was consistent over social class, and also influenced how the product was rated.

Another aspect of the relationship between the source and the message is found in the sleeper effect, which is described in Chapter 2 on propaganda.

Message

Some of the many features that have been found to be important in the content of messages include:

- *one- or two-sided messages*: the research suggests that if the audience is already on your side it is best to give a one-sided argument, but if they are not on your side it is better to consider alternative viewpoints as well as your own.
- *stating conclusions*: a message appears to be most effective if you clearly state the conclusions of the message rather than letting your audience work it out for themselves.
- *fear arousal*: many messages contain some element of fear (for example, suggestions that people will think you smell if you do not use deodorants), but research on this going as far back as Janis and Feshbach (1953) found that fear arousal is more likely to make people avoid the message than respond to it.

Medium

Messages can be given face to face, or through television, or through radio, or through print. Chaiken and Eagly (1983) found that audio-visual messages have a greater effect on attitudes and behaviour than do print messages. They also discovered that the likeability of the source is more important in audio-visual messages than it is in print. When we read a message we find it easier to dissociate the content of the message from the source of the message. In fact, we are often not conscious of who is the source of a written message.

Target

Different audiences respond to different messages. It is important, therefore, to target your message for a particular audience. One rather sinister example of this comes from the American tobacco companies, who specifically targeted Black and Hispanic Americans in their campaigns during the 1970s and 1980s (Zimbardo and Leippe 1991). Over the next thirty years, cancer rates for Black and Hispanic Americans rose much faster than the rates for White Americans. The campaigns were used to target minority groups in America, developing brands specifically aimed at minority groups and advertising heavily in magazines with Black and Hispanic readers. Targeting is an important part of many advertising campaigns, and a further example is described later in this chapter on the Lucozade campaign.

Situation

It is one of the consistent findings of social psychology that situations affect behaviour (for example, see Orne, 1962 on **demand characteristics**). Messages sound different depending where you hear or read them. For example, a message for a health product is unlikely to be well received by people relaxing in front of a television with their evening meal. The effectiveness of the message depends, in part, on our readiness to receive it.

Mathur and Chattopadhyay (1991) showed how the mood of the viewer affects the effectiveness of an advertisement. They looked at how the mood of an advert interacted with the mood of a television programme. The study discovered that the mood of the programme affected how people viewed the advertisement and how much of it they remembered. Happy programmes encouraged more recall of the advertisements. If people were in a sombre mood, they appeared to recall less of the promotional messages. This would explain the position of public service announcements at the end of an advertising segment. Public service announcements such as 'Dip Your Headlights!' are designed to create a thoughtful and sombre response, and this would interfere with the other messages if it appeared at the beginning of the advertising segment.

Factoids

We like to believe that our attitudes are based on reason and good sense, and that we consider the appropriate evidence before coming to our conclusions about someone or something. This is not always the case, and sometimes we put undue faith in factoids. Factoids are 'facts which have no existence before appearing in a magazine or newspaper' (Norman Mailer, cited in Pratkanis and Aronson, 1992, p. 71). An example of this in the area of consumer choice comes from a leaflet circulated in France and referred to as the 'Leaflet of Villejuif' (see Kapferer, 1989). The leaflet, whose source is unknown, was produced in simple type, photocopied and handed around. It said that a number of mass-produced drinks such as Coca Cola should be avoided because they contain carcinogens (substances that cause cancer).

The leaflet claimed to come from the hospital of Villejuif, which has a reputation for its cancer work. The hospital, however denies all knowledge of the leaflet and says the details on the leaflet are incorrect. Despite this, the leaflet has been widely circulated (around half the population report they have read or heard of the leaflet, 19 per cent said they had stopped buying the products mentioned in the leaflet, and many more said they intended to stop buying them). This is an example of how a product can be damaged by a factoid, but the more common case involves advertisers creating factoids to change our behaviour. These factoids often include scientific-looking graphics which show, for example, how a painkiller works (even though research suggests that we have little understanding of this process), or how a shampoo affects your hair.

The psychology of consumers

A good starting point in the history of psychology's relationship with consumers is the change in career forced on the behaviourist John Watson in 1920. Despite his academic achievements, Watson was unable to obtain a post in a university and was forced to earn a living in the commercial world. He joined the marketing company J. Walter Thompson and rose from selling coffee to become a Vice President of the company (see Cohen, 1979). His contribution to marketing was the introduction of the rigorous research techniques that were being developed in psychology. Since that time, psychologists have become increasingly involved in the world of marketing and advertising.

Research on consumer behaviour has come up with five 'facts' about the effectiveness of advertising messages in Western societies (Pratkanis and Aronson, 1992):

* Advertisements that contain the following words – new, quick, improved, now, suddenly, amazing, introducing – sell more products.
* Products placed at eye level in supermarkets sell best.
* Advertisements that feature babies, or animals, or have something to do with sex appeal, are more effective at selling than advertisements that use cartoon characters or historical figures.
* Products at the end of aisles or near checkouts in supermarkets sell better than those placed elsewhere.
* Putting items in bundles – for example, 2 for £1, rather than 1 for 50 pence – can increase the purchasers judgment of their 'value for money'.

These five facts do not come from theory but from observation of consumer behaviour. It is not clear why consumers behave in this way, and so psychology tries to come up with explanations of this behaviour.

In this section we will look at four features of the relationship between psychology and consumers:

1. *Developing a need*: if we do not want a product or believe that we need it, then we will never buy it.
2. *Noticing the product*: the product needs to stand out from all the others that are available.
3. *Purchasing the product*: even when we are aware of a product and want to own it, we do not always decide to buy it.
4. *Behaviour after the purchase*: after we have bought the product we might decide to make a repeat purchase or maybe recommend it to someone else.

Figure 3.2 **One of the first coffee break advertisements**

Developing a need

The starting point for selling a product would seem to be convincing people that they want it or, even better, they need it. Sometimes people do not even know they need it until they are convinced by advertising. For example, according to Mullen and Johnson (1990), the accepted idea of having a 'coffee break' is largely attributed to an advertising campaign launched by the Joint Coffee Trade Publicity Committee (in the USA) during the 1920s (see Figure 3.2). This campaign created the idea that breaks are pleasant social events that aid work, rest and play. Refreshment breaks are now an accepted part of life, and this means that we will buy and consume some food products during these breaks. A social need was created that can only be satisfied by consumption. 'Have a break – have a sit down and a think' doesn't sound quite right. To have a 'proper' break we have to consume something.

One of the most effective ways of creating a need is to play on our sense of social embarrassment. If we can make people embarrassed about something, then we can sell them something to remove this embarrassment. For example, during the 1920s the makers of Listerine (mouthwash) popularised the term halitosis to refer to bad breath. Until this time, most people were not aware of the term or the problem. The advertisers plugged into the paranoia of our social embarrassment by saying that 'even your best friends won't tell you'. On a similar theme, the term 'BO' (or body odour) was invented for a campaign to promote Lifebuoy soap (Fox, 1984).

Subliminal perception

Making people want something seems an obvious process in advertising, but is it possible to give people a motivational message without them knowing it? Psychologists discovered that people can register and respond to messages without being aware of them. This is called **subliminal perception**, and it offers a lot of potential for advertisers, but only if it works. Subliminal messages are messages that are too weak to reach conscious awareness, perhaps because they occur too rapidly, or are too faint. Not surprisingly, this is a very controversial area and the research about the effectiveness of this technique is rather inconclusive.

A famous example of an attempt to use this technique is provided by in a paper by Brean (1958) which described a market researcher who arranged with a cinema owner for the use of second special projector to deliver subliminal messages. This projector flashed the words 'EAT POPCORN' and 'DRINK COCA-COLA' on to the screen every five seconds during the showing of a regular film. The exposure was extremely brief, only 1/3000th of a second, which is well below the ordinary human perceptual threshold for visual information, so the cinema-goers were unaware that the information had been transmitted.

They showed this subliminal message to over 45,000 people during the six-week trial period. During that trial, sales of Coca-Cola at the cinema rose by 18 per cent and popcorn sales rose by nearly 60 per cent. However, the details of the study are not well reported and the film itself (*Picnic*) contained several scenes of eating and drinking, so it is uncertain how far the effect really came from the subliminal message. A second trial, in which the words 'ICE CREAM' were presented subliminally shortly before the cinema interval, was reported to have produced a rise in sales of ice cream, but also a number of complaints to the management that the cinema was too cold!

The jury is out on the effectiveness of subliminal advertisements, and Zimbardo and Leippe (1991) suggest that some of the research, including the above study, is fairly suspect. There was enough concern about subliminals, however, to ensure they were banned in both the USA and the UK. Zimbardo and Lieppe reviewed the laboratory evidence on subliminals and concluded that there is a clear, though weak, effect produced by visual presentations. However, they went on to suggest that there is little or no effect from hidden messages in print or radio presentations. Although subliminals do not appear to be very effective, advertisers can use other ways of getting messages across, and sometimes these too can be so subtle as to operate unconsciously on the consumer. The use of colour and visual images in advertisements are very carefully selected so as to evoke moods, associations and impressions, as is the use of background music in supermarkets (see below).

Noticing the product

Memory for the message is an important consideration for advertisers. If we hear the message often enough then we will remember it. Well, not exactly. The evidence suggests that repetition is not a good strategy for learning. This is illustrated by Bekerian and Baddeley's study of housewives' (their term) memory for radio frequencies. In 1980 the BBC changed the frequencies of all its major radio stations, and carried out a campaign to give maximum exposure to the new frequencies using radio, television and poster displays. Bekerian and Baddeley (1980) estimated that the housewives in their study had each heard the new wavelengths about a thousand times. But when they were asked to recall these frequencies, either by writing down the numbers or by marking a dial, only about a quarter could do so. Simple repetition without processing, apparently, is remarkably

Figure 3.3 Advertisement presenting different messages to left and right visual fields

ineffective. Advertisers therefore try to get us to process the information in some way by, for example, associating the product with an everyday event, or by making us think about the advertisement, or by showing several versions of the same advertisement.

When we view advertisements on television, we often have the choice to avoid them by 'zapping' to another channel (though only if you have been able to win control of the remote), or by 'zipping' through the video on fast-forward. Olney, Holbrook and Batra (1991) looked at how people pay attention to advertisements, and in particular at whether people's attitudes had an effect on their attention. People were asked to watch a series of advertisements and the researchers measured how much they paid attention to them by recording the viewing time of various adverts, in terms of 'zipping' and 'zapping'. Not surprisingly, the researchers found that the uniqueness of the advertisement had a great effect on the attention levels. Advertisements which created emotions in the viewer were linked with high levels of attention, but those which contained a lot of facts were avoided. The study also showed that emotion provoking images and situations were more efficient in capturing the viewer's attention than information about the product. This might explain the trend in advertising for obscure images and very little, if any, mention of the product.

The way that we look at advertisements and process the information might also have an affect on our response to the message. The structure of the visual system means that information from the right side of a visual image is processed by the left hemisphere of the brain, while that from the left side of the image is processed by the right hemisphere. Some physiological research suggests that the left side of the brain appears to be dominant in language functions, whereas the right hemisphere is more dominant in spatial and imagination tasks, and possibly emotions (although that last point is more contentious). Horowitz and Kaye (1975) suggested that the implication of this is that the most effective advertisements will have text on the right side of the display, and emotional and spatial features on the left side of the display like the one shown in Figure 3.3

Classical conditioning

One concept from psychology that particularly lends itself to modern advertising is **classical conditioning**. The basic idea is to establish an association between a product and a pleasant feeling. One way of doing this is to show the product with pictures that create an 'aahhh' response. Babies usually produce this response in adults, as do young animals like puppies. The relevance of a Labrador puppy to toilet paper is negligible (except for when it is used to clear up 'accidents'), but the puppy produces an 'aahhh' response and encourages the viewer to associate warm feelings with the brand name of toilet paper. So effective is this advertisement that there will be very few readers who cannot name or recognise that brand of toilet paper. Advertisers obviously believe that it works, but is their any research evidence to support this belief?

A study on this idea was carried out by Stayman and Batra (1991), who looked at how emotional states affect memory for a product and also affect the purchase choice of a product. During a television programme, people were shown a short advertisement which was either 'informational' or 'emotional' in style. Later, the same people were asked to make a brand choice between two similar products. Stayman and Batra found that those people who had seen the emotional advert were more likely to choose that product than those who had seen the informational advertisement.

The evidence suggests that advertisers can bypass our minds and appeal directly to our emotions. You might like to observe how many advertisements use this technique of trying to make you feel positive about their product by associating it with cute and cuddly pictures or exciting music or mildly amusing images.

Purchasing the product

Another concept from learning theory used by advertisers is called the **imitation effect**. This is concerned with how quickly a new product will be adopted by consumers. If it is successfully adopted, their rate of purchase typically shows a curve which is gentle at first, but then rises ever more steeply. This is explained in terms of the way that a relatively small number of people are likely to adopt a new product in the first place, but if they do accept it and it becomes fashionable, others will imitate and follow their example.

In view of the imitation effect, it is pretty important that some people should obtain the opportunity to adopt a new product easily and quickly. An example of how this can affect sales was demonstrated by the innovation of Post-it Notes (see Thompson, 1984). These little stick-on sheets seem to be everywhere now, but the initial marketing through the conventional route of office supply stores was not very successful. In Denver and Tulsa (in the USA), however, the dealers ran promotions which involved giving out free samples of the product, and this was much more successful. The company therefore decided to perform a market test in a town, in which samples were mailed out to every office in the city. Since these were free, the employees also took them home. The result of this was that not just office workers, but also their families and friends began to demand the product, creating a market for widespread distribution.

In the mood

Another way to enhance sales is to create the right mood in shoppers, and one technique for this is to use background music. An investigation into background music (Milliman, 1982) compared the effects of several different types of music in an American supermarket over a nine-week period. The background music varied between slow tempo music, fast tempo music, and no music at all. Milliman found that shoppers moved at a different pace, depending on the tempo of the music. In addition, sales went up by nearly 40 per cent when slow tempo music was playing. By moving more slowly, shoppers spent more time in the store and purchased more products. When you shop in a major supermarket today, nothing is left to chance. The design of the shelves, the position of various products, the smells and the music of the shop are all carefully controlled.

The supermarket is designed so that you will buy more products, but how do manufacturers encourage you to buy their particular products rather than those of their competitors? With so many advertisements bombarding us with information every day, it is important to have some trick to help us remember the message when we are in the shop. One trick is to use memory **retrieval cues** to enhance memory for a particular product. One way of activating some retrieval cues is to place pictures from television advertising on the packaging of the product. Laboratory and field research has suggested that this can be very effective, particularly in helping people to recall the advertisement's claims. The Campbell Soup Company, for example, reported that sales increased by 15 per cent when their point-of-sales materials (promotional materials in supermarkets) were directly related to their television advertising (Keller, 1987).

Behaviour after the purchase

It's not all over for the advertiser once the product has been purchased. It is often important to encourage repeat purchases. To do this with, for example, food products, it is necessary to encourage the person to consume the food as often as possible. This was achieved by an innovative campaign from Kellogg's Corn Flakes in 1981 (Elliot, 1984). Kellogg's (in conjunction with their advertising agency, J. Walter Thompson) decided to place their advertisement on as many breakfast tables as possible by printing it on one million milk bottles. The milk bottles of Unigate Dairies have an average 'life' of twenty-eight trips, so the advertisers were able to calculate that the advertisement would reach three million doorsteps on average nine times each.

The campaign was very effective in terms of increasing use among existing purchasers, but it did not increase the market penetration of Corn Flakes. That is, people who were not currently using Corn Flakes were not encouraged to go out and buy them. However, people who already had Corn Flakes in their larders ate more of them and subsequently bought more of them. In fact the advertisers estimated that homes receiving the Unigate milk bottles increased their purchases of Corn Flakes by 17 per cent.

Another psychological concept that describes our after-purchase experience is **cognitive dissonance** (see Festinger 1957). According to this theory, once we have decided to make a purchase, we will justify that decision to ourselves by enhancing our opinion of the product. So if we chose to buy a Twinky Washing Machine rather than a Spinky Washing Machine, we are likely to believe that it is much better appliance, and bore all our friends by telling them about it. In a study of car buyers, Ehrlich *et al.* (1957) interviewed 125 men in an advertising survey to find out which car advertisements they read. Sixty-five of the men had recently bought new cars. They found that new car owners tended to read advertisements about the make of car which they had bought much more often than advertisements for other types of car. They also observed that the owners of new cars generally tended to read fewer car advertisements than other people. Ehrlich *et al.* suggested that the new car owners were trying to achieve cognitive consistency by looking for information that backed up their purchase choice, and by avoiding information which might challenge it.

Progress exercise

Make yourself comfortable and watch some television (oh go on, it's for your own good!). Record a small batch of advertisements. Watch them through a few times and identify as many psychological techniques as you can. You might consider

- What is the advertisement trying to make you think?
- What is the advertisement trying to make you feel?
- What is the advertisement trying to make you do?

The psychology of products

An important part of advertising is knowing the psychology of the product. How does the consumer view the product and why do they buy it? An interesting example of the importance of matching the product to the consumer comes from the sale of cake mixes in the 1960s. When instant cake mixes first appeared on the shelves they were not very popular. These cakes mixes were intended to simplify home-baking of cakes, and required the cook to just add water. Unfortunately, women, who were the major purchasers of cake mixes, did not like that. However, when the company changed its recipe, so that the cook had to add an egg to the mixture, sales increased dramatically (Myers and Reynolds 1967).

We can explain this rather puzzling finding by looking at the expectations of what you should do when you are cooking. For many of us, cooking means piercing the plastic lid, but in the 1950s and early 1960s it was taken for granted that regular cake-making was a routine part of womanly tasks, and many women found the ability to produce a good cake an important visible sign that they were good at their job of housekeeping. A mixture which reduced the activity to simply adding water did not allow any sense of involvement. However, if they had to beat an egg and add it to the mixture, it seemed much more like 'real' cooking. This allowed the cook to feel that they had actively taken part in the baking process, and deserved some of the credit for the outcome. Although it may seem trivial to a modern society in which bought cakes have become the norm, the ability to make good cakes was at that time important in satisfying self-esteem needs, and this was reflected in the purchasing behaviour of women.

Expectation also has an effect on our acceptance of products. Our regular experience of a product leads us to believe that this is how the product should be. For example, Schrank (1977) described the 'pineapple juice bias', which refers to the observation that the taste most Americans associate with pineapple juice is usually an artificial flavour. This is because most pineapple juice consumed in America is from cans and the flavour is influenced by the metallic taste of the can, pineapple flavouring agents and artificial sweeteners. After a lifetime of experience with canned pineapple, the person who tries fresh pineapple for the first time might think there is something wrong with it. I experienced the same effect the first time I had a 'real' Bakewell tart in Bakewell, Derbyshire. The recipe for this delicacy is secret to a few people in the village and so the only authentic Bakewell tarts come from Bakewell. However, pale imitations have flooded the market over the years so that when I had my first 'real' example I thought it was not a 'proper' Bakewell tart (this part of the book is sponsored by the Derbyshire Tourist Board).

Our expectations might lead us to accept no alternative to the real thing. The real thing, as the jingle goes, is Coca-Cola, and for years the Coca-Cola company fiercely protected the recipe for the drink so that they could claim it had an exclusive taste. The recipe, however, was discovered in documents from the Coca-Cola company by Pendergrast (1993) during some research into the company. Pendergrast asked Coca Cola what would be the effect of publishing it and, surprisingly, their advertising executive did not seem to fear any competition. The executive said 'We're selling smoke. They're drinking the image, not the product.'

One of the concerns of market research has been to discover the motives behind consumption of various products, and therefore a better means of selling the product. One result of this research is to develop a typology which is designed to indicate a type of person who has a particular set of motivations. This typology can then be used to target advertisements more effectively. For example, Ackoff and Emshoff (1975) identified four general 'types' of drinkers, with different motivations for drinking.

Ackoff and Emshoff recruited a number of beer drinkers to take part in a study based on this approach. Each drinker took a test that categorised them as one of the four types. They were then shown four commercials for four different brands of beer. Each commercial followed a similar pattern, but had been made with one of the personality types in mind. The first segment of each commercial introduced the main character and identified them as one of the motivational types. This was followed by a second segment that showed the actor drinking and a finally third segment that showed a change in behaviour in line with the motivation for drinking. So, for example, the commercial featuring the Oceanic Drinker showed the actor becoming more extroverted.

After seeing the commercials, the drinkers were asked to sample the four beers shown – although the only difference between them was name and packaging – and asked to choose a case of one of the 'brands' to take home as a reward for participating in the study. Ackoff and Emshoff reported that the drinkers consistently expressed a preference for the beer that was associated with their motivational type. Most of the drinkers were sure they could tell the brands apart, and most described at least one of the brands as not fit for human

Table 3.1 Motivational 'types' of drinkers	
1 The Oceanic Drinker:	tends to drink so as to become more gregarious and extroverted.
2 The Indulgent Drinker:	tends to drink in order to become withdrawn and introverted.
3 The Reparative Drinker:	tends to drink in order to wind down from work and ease into leisure, and also reward themselves for all their efforts.
4 The Social Drinker:	tends to use alcohol as a social lubricant.

Source: Ackoff and Emshoff (1975)

consumption, despite the fact that they were drinking exactly the same beer!

Naming

Choosing the right name for a product can make all the difference to its success. One suggestion is that they should be easy to visualise and therefore easy to remember. This was learned by the American Matex Corporation, who had developed a product for inhibiting rust and began by marketing it under the name of 'Thixo-Tex'. Sales were extremely disappointing. After some discussion, according to White (1980) the product was remarketed as 'Rusty Jones'. As a result, sales rose enormously, from $2 million worth of sales in 1976 to $100 million worth of sales in 1980.

Product names can also have disastrous effects on sales. The American company Gerber was famous for its baby foods and tried to repeat its success in the adult market. It introduced adult meals such as Beef Burgundy and Mediterranean Vegetables and put them in a jar that looked much like its baby food. This was probably a tactical mistake, but it compounded the problem by calling the product 'Singles'. Later research showed that even though many adults eat alone they do not want to be classified in that way. They could only have made it worse by calling it 'Billy No-Mates Meals' (reported in Mullen and Johnson, 1990).

Naming has some generalisation effects. Ries and Trout (1981) observed that some organisations attempt to increase the awareness of one product by associating it to a family of other products. This can be achieved by attaching the company name to a range of different items. For example, the Virgin Company started out as a music production company but now brands all manner of products including soft drinks, insurance policies, shops, trains and planes. We expect some connection between these different products, and depending on your attitudes towards Virgin you will either purchase a lot or none of these. Generalisation of the product can have the effect of making us use a particular product name for a range of products. For example, when we go to clear up the place we live in we might say 'Where's the Hoover?', meaning 'where is the vacuum cleaner?'. Hoover is, of course, a brand name and refers to only some of the vacuum cleaners bought every year. We are, however, likely to think about 'hoovering' the house (though rarely likely to actually do it) and this shows how successful the Hoover Company has been in promoting its product.

Naming is believed to be so important to the success of a product that there are a number of companies that specialise in picking names. Companies such as Name Lab and The Name Works will charge a substantial sum for several weeks work picking a name. An example of their work is given in Engel *et al.* (1990) who described how a company was set up to sell portable computers. It was originally going to be called 'Gateway', but after consultation with a naming company changed the name to 'Compaq'. This name was selected from a short list of suggestions including 'Cortex', 'Cognipak' and 'Suntek'. You will notice that 'Compaq' is made up of two syllables that each suggest some meaning. One implies computers and the other implies communications. Together they sound a little like 'compact'. It is not possible to estimate the effect of the name, but it is interesting to note that the company sales for the initial twelve months were an American record for first-year sales.

The selling of Lucozade

Lucozade is a glucose carbonated drink first made in the 1920s. The drink is a highly concentrated source of energy which is quickly assimilated into the bloodstream. It is easily digested, and its flavour, carbonation and relative sweetness make it easy to take when you are sick. During the period 1974 to 1978, the sales of Lucozade declined consistently. The advertising strategy promoted Lucozade as a unique source of liquid energy that helps the family when they are recovering from illness. In all the advertisements, the emotional way of showing the family was through children. As a result the drink had a very clear market image, but that image was restricted to being a product that was associated with children, illness and occasional use.

Rather surprisingly, the market research showed that only 20 per cent of the sales were for convalescence, and only 30 per cent were being drunk by children. A substantial volume of the drink was being consumed by healthy adults. Basically, the bottle was being bought when there was a sick child in the house but it was then being drunk by other members of the household. If we look at the Yale model of communication (see above) and apply it to this example, we can see that the source of the message of the advertisements was about child health and the target of the adverts was parents (mainly mothers).

The problem with this approach was that the drink was being consumed in other circumstances and this was not being reinforced by the advertising campaign. A further problem was that children were

Lucozade
Ups and Downs.

MAN: How often do you start out feeling full of get-up-and-go and then…

after you've been working hard, you start to slow down.

That's the time to sit down and have a glass of Lucozade. Lucozade's not just refreshing…

it provides glucose energy in the most natural form the body can use.

So, before you get up and get going again, have some Lucozade.

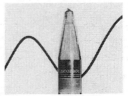

SINGERS: Lucozade refreshes you through the ups and downs of the day.

***Figure 3.4* The Lucozade campaign**
Source: Leo Burnett Advertising Agency

generally getting healthier and so the usual reason for buying Lucozade was not there as often. The solution was to 're-position' the product as a health drink rather than a sickness drink. The first campaign to start this change is shown in Figure 3.4.

The campaign was very successful, so much so that many adults still recognise the tune and message today. Measures at the time showed that in contrast to the previous sales decline, the first year of the campaign showed a 13 per cent increase in volume sales. Market research also showed an increase in the number of people claiming to buy Lucozade 'nowadays', an increase in the number of people giving 'refreshment' as a reason for purchase, and an increase in the recall of Lucozade television advertising.

The campaign changed perceptions of Lucozade so that instead of it being a sickness product it became a health product. Since this campaign, Lucozade has further developed that theme and now markets itself as a sports drink giving high energy. This campaign shows how it is important to understand public perceptions of a product and match any advertising campaign to those perceptions.

Summary

Psychology has been studying the effectiveness of advertisements for around one hundred years. During that time it has been able to identify a number of effective techniques that encourage people to buy certain products. It has not, however, been possible to identify the way that people make all their decisions, and so advertising still remains largely a process of trial and error.

Review exercise

Design an advertising campaign for a new product designed to reduce foot odour. Use the psychological concepts from this chapter to do the following:

• Name the product
• Design the packaging
• Suggest a slogan
• Identify where you will place your advertisements

Further reading

Broadbent, S. (1984) *Twenty Advertising Case Histories*, London: Holt, Rinehart. Fascinating accounts of successful advertising campaigns selling products such as boxes of matches and frozen fish.

Mullen, B. and Johnson, C. (1990) *The Psychology of Consumer Behaviour*, New Jersey: Lawrence Erlbaum Associates. A readable account of the main themes of consumer psychology with lots of examples.

4

Bias in psychology

Introduction

It is interesting that we have a title such as 'bias in psychology'. It seems obvious to me that everything in psychology contains some sort of bias or other, but what is remarkable is that this bias is often not acknowledged. Perhaps this is because one feature of the scientific approach in psychology is the attempt to be objective. To be objective is usually taken to mean standing apart from the subject that is being studied, and being free from bias. This might be possible if we are studying chemicals or micro-organisms, but is it possible to be objective when we are studying the behaviour and experience of people? It is difficult, if not impossible, to stand apart from the subject that is being studied when the subject is human behaviour and experience and you are a human being. In this chapter we will look at some examples of bias in psychology, and pay particular attention to issues around cultural diversity and gender. We will start by looking at the concept of ethnocentrism.

Ethnocentrism

One source of bias in psychology comes from the fact that we tend to see things from our own viewpoint and the viewpoint of people like us. In our everyday lives we are asked to make judgments about people and events. We have a range of opinions that we are prepared to offer to other people when asked, and sometimes when not asked. In our judgments we are often inclined to show a little egocentrism (seeing things from our own particular viewpoint to the exclusion of others). Another bias that can affect our judgments is **ethnocentrism** (seeing things from the point of view of our group).

Ethnocentrism can be defined as the following syndrome of behaviours:

(a) a tendency to under-value the out-group's products
(b) an increased rejection and hostility towards out-group members
(c) a tendency to over-value the in-group's products
(d) an increased liking for in-group members (accompanied by pressures for conformity and group cohesion)

(LeVine and Campbell, 1972)

From an ethnocentric standpoint, we tend to see our own team as being best. Also, we underestimate the errors and failings in our own team and exaggerate them in the opposing team. There are a number of reasons for this, including our access to evidence. We are likely to know far more about the behaviour and opinions of people with whom we mix and people who are like us. Also, if we support people like ourselves then we are likely to receive support back from these people. We expect our friends to support us and not to do us down, particularly in the company of strangers. It is all to do with social cohesion and a sense of belonging.

The downside of the ethnocentric outlook is that we are likely to show **prejudice** towards people who are not like us and not in our group. The early psychological theories of prejudice suggested that it came from childhood experiences and only affected a small minority of people. The theory of the authoritarian personality, for example, put forward by Adorno *et al.* (1950) described prejudice as a consequence of a failure to resolve childhood conflicts between children and their parents. More recent descriptions of prejudice by, for example Tajfel (1970), suggest that we make prejudiced judgements and actions on the basis of our group membership. This approach would suggest that this ethnocentric bias is an inevitable part of social living. The task for us then becomes to be aware of our ethnocentric bias and try to acknowledge the worth of people who are not in our group.

How does ethnocentrism affect psychology?

Ethnocentrism means that we give undue prominence to our own group of people. An analysis of introductory text books by Smith and Bond (1993) found that they mainly cited work by researchers from America. In a fairly standard American text by Baron and Byrne (1991), 94 per cent of the 1,700 studies mentioned were in fact from America. In a British text (Hewstone *et al.*, 1988), about 66 per cent of the studies were American, 32 per cent were European and under 2 per cent came from the rest of the world. These books are by no means exceptional, and they reflect the places where psychological research is conducted. It is estimated by Rosenzweig (cited in Smith and Bond, 1993) that there are 56,000 psychology researchers in the world and about 64 per cent of them are American. So, psychological research is mainly conducted by American and Europeans, and they mainly study themselves. This means that the psychology in our text books is the psychology of Americans and Europeans, but it is by no means clear whether the behaviour these people display is the same behaviour we can expect in other cultures and other lifestyles. This means we have two possible sources of bias: (i) researchers mainly study their own culture, and (b) researchers find it difficult to interpret the behaviour and experience of people from other cultures.

Matsumoto (1994) suggested there are five main reasons why American psychology is ethnocentric:

1   it is mainly interested in Americans;
2   the organisations who offer research funds are not primarily interested in other peoples;

3   the choice of subjects (participants) is often based on availability (see the description of Sears, 1986 in Chapter 6), and this means students in higher education;

4   research into other peoples might come up with some uncomfortable findings and this could have political consequences;

5   the researchers are mainly White Americans from the professional classes.

Matsumoto suggests that this ethnocentric approach is being challenged by the change in the profile of students in American universities, the change in the profile of psychology research staff and a growing awareness in psychology, and society in general, of our ethnocentrism.

Can we be objective?

A problem for psychology is that it attempts to adopt a detached academic and 'scientific' standpoint. Scientists pretend to be objective, that is, free from bias and free from value. But this cannot be so. As we have seen above, you inevitably view the world from a particular perspective, that of yourself and the various groups to which you belong. I cannot be free from bias because my behaviour and conversation are affected by the way I interpret the world and the opinions that frame these interpretations.

Sometimes psychologists attempt to take a balanced view. The problem with this attempt is that it presumes that we all agree where the middle of two opposing arguments, and hence the balance, should lie. To take an extreme example, imagine taking a balanced approach to child sexual abuse. Should we position ourselves midway between someone who opposes adult–child sexual contact and someone who advocates it (a paedophile)? This a clearly a nonsense. So we have to accept that the choice of the balancing point is not a matter of detached objectivity, but a matter of opinion.

Balance and objectivity are not possible. What is important is to be aware of your perspective and the limitations it imposes on your view. Psychology, unfortunately, is often blind to its perspectives and their biases. In the next section we will go on to look at three sources of bias in psychology that come from the way it carries out its investigations;

average people, the differences between and within groups, and invisible people.

Average people

A large number of psychological studies are designed to look for measures of differences between groups of people or between conditions. These studies rarely look at individual diversity as one of the key features. It is more common for the 'subjects'[1] to be treated as identical people and for the 'subject variables' (psychology-speak for our individuality) to be kept to a minimum or ignored. This means that the conclusions of the research can only produce statements about how 'most people' or the 'average person' will behave. But who is this average person, and what does he or she think, feel and do? And, is it reasonable to assume that most people are 'average'?

Engineering psychologists (ergonomists) measure the dimensions of different parts of the body to see what is the best possible design for machinery. Designing a car seat is a good example. The seat needs to be comfortable for most people that would want to drive the car. The obvious strategy would be to design the seat for the '50th percentile person', the person who is average on all, or almost all, of the body dimensions. The dimensions include standing height, sitting height, arm reach, knee height, shoulder breadth and so on. It is unlikely that any one person would be exactly average on a whole battery of dimensions, but we could reasonably expect a number of people to be in the middle third of most dimensions. Unfortunately, this is not so. A study by Daniels (cited in Gregory and Burroughs, 1989, p. 65) investigated the body dimensions of 4,000 flying personnel on just ten dimensions. They found that not one person fell in the middle third for all measurements. Nobody had an average body, or to put it another way, there was no average person.

---

1 There is some controversy over whether to use the term 'subject' or 'participant' to describe the people who are studied in psychological investigations. In my opinion it is only appropriate to describe someone as a participant if they have some say in what is going on and have some ownership of the data. If they are just brought into the laboratory and have things done to them and measures taken from them, then the best term to describe them is probably 'subjects'.

Another example of this individual diversity can be seen in the diagrams of stomachs shown below (Figure 4.1). A comparison of the drawings of twelve 'real' stomachs with a text-book drawing of a 'normal stomach' shows that none of the stomachs are 'normal' and many do not even look like stomachs.

If there is no such thing as an average body, it seems rather unlikely that there is such a thing as an average personality or an average behaviour pattern. When we talk about averages we mean that we

A "textbook" stomach

I   II   III   IV

V   VI   VII   VIII

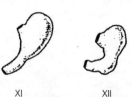

IX   X   XI   XII

Figure 4.1 **The 'average' stomach and real stomachs**

have added up all the scores and divided by the number of measurements taken. This average score does not have to describe the behaviour or personality of even one person. So, when psychology texts and research papers talk about how people behave, they are referring to a theoretical average person, and it might well be that no real person actually behaves like this.

Differences between groups and within groups

One of the problems that comes from looking at average scores is that you can come to some inappropriate conclusions about group differences. For example, there is a lot of interest in the differences in performance between men and women. If you take the average score of men on some dimension and compare it with the average score of women you might find a small difference. However, the spread of scores among men and women far outweighs the difference between the two groups. Also, with regard to gender differences in children, for example, reviews of the research into cognitive ability and social behaviour have consistently found that there are very few measurable differences, and in the cases where there is a difference the effect is very small (for example, Woolley, 1910, cited in Williams, 1987; Maccoby and Jacklin, 1974).

Look at the example distributions below (Figure 4.2). They show the different distributions of boys and girls on a made-up variable of 'binkiness'. You will see that girls have an average binkiness score a little higher than boys, but that the distributions overlap so much that it would be impossible to predict a person's binkiness score just by knowing their gender. An analysis of the research on the development of social and cognitive behaviour found that male–female difference accounted for only 1–5 per cent of the variance in the population (Deaux, 1984). This means that gender is a very poor predictor of how an individual will behave.

Invisible people

A further problem with the idea of the 'average person' is that some groups of people are excluded. Any minority group is, by definition, going to have only a small effect on the average. These groups of people are therefore excluded from the discussions about behaviour

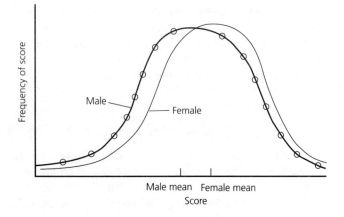

Figure 4.2 **Distributions of 'binkiness' in boys and girls**

and experience. For example, the majority of people in this country have mainly heterosexual relationships, but a significant minority have same-sex relationships. The 'average person' is clearly hetero-sexual, but if we just describe the behaviour of these average people we are ignoring the behaviour and experience of a significant minority.

Our concepts of average or normal behaviour contain a number of assumptions and biases. A study by Broverman *et al.* (1971) into what doctors expect of healthy people illustrates this problem. In this survey, doctors were asked to identify the terms that best described (a) a healthy adult, (b) a healthy man, or (c) a healthy woman. There was good agreement between the doctors on what were the characteristics of each group. The characteristics of the healthy man were judged to be very similar to the characteristics of a healthy adult, which is what we would expect. The characteristics of a healthy woman, however, were significantly different from the characteristics of the healthy adult. One of the inferences we can draw from this is that when doctors think of an 'adult' they are assuming that it is male. Although the term appears neutral, it carries some hidden assumptions and biases.

So, there are adults and there are also women. If we take this a step further, I would suggest that there are also the following assumptions in our language:

- there are people and there are Black people;
- there are people and there are gays and lesbians;
- there are people and there are disabled people.

I could go on, but I do not want to labour the point. We need to be aware, then, that apparently neutral terms like 'people' actually contain a lot of assumptions.

When we use the term people, we do not mean 'all people' but just 'average people'. What this means is that a large number of people are invisible in psychology texts. In fact, we do not even notice that they are absent. This would not matter if the experiences of these people were the same as the experiences of the 'average person', but unfortunately, they are not. The problem for psychology is that if these invisible people are to be included, the results of studies and the structure of theories might be very different. We will come back to this point later in this chapter when we look at some replications of famous studies carried out in countries other than the original.

Summary

To put the above in a nutshell,

- the average person does not exist, and referring to averages of behaviour and experience masks the differences between individuals;
- the perceived differences between groups of people are based on differences in average scores, and these differences are often much smaller than the differences between individuals within the groups;
- by reducing 'subject variables' and looking at average performance some groups of people are made invisible within psychology.

Racism in psychology

Psychology has some unconscious biases that we can see as ethnocentrism, but there are also some examples of work in psychology that can be called racist. In the next section we will look at implicit racism, scientific racism, and the study of prejudice.

Implicit racism

One of the debates that creates a lot of controversy is the idea of freedom of speech. The argument is sometimes put forward that people should be allowed to publish objectionable material because it is important to allow everyone to have their say. This argument is sometimes used to support the publication of racist material in a wide range of situations including academic psychology. One question that is worth considering is whether this idea of freedom of speech hides a number of other biases and assumptions.

A study by MaCullough (1988) challenged the notion of freedom of speech. In this study, students were presented with a two-section booklet to complete. One section contained information about the 'Sexual Liberation Party' which advocated legalising sex between adults and children. The other section had information about the National Front (an openly racist political organisation). After reading the information about each organisation, the subjects were asked to respond to the idea that the government should ban the organisation. The two descriptions of the organisation were very similar with a few key words exchanged: Blacks/children, racism/sexual abuse, racists/paedophiles.

The experiment was designed to test the hypothesis that the general failure of White people to respond to racism is not due to libertarian ideas about free speech, but to **implicit racism**. The evidence supported this notion of implicit racism because the students were more willing to ban the Sexual Liberation Party than to ban the National Front. The hypothesis was also supported by the editors of *The Psychologist* in their choice of title for the article: 'Are WE secret racists?'. Who is the 'we' in this title? The editors were clearly assuming that their audience (the 'we') was exclusively White. The title was not suggested by the author, but the editors of *The Psychologist*.

Scientific racism

A further example of implicit racism was shown by the decision of *The Psychologist* to publish an article by Rushton (1990). In this article, Rushton proposed a modern theory of 'racial differences' that attempted to put forward an evolutionary explanation. There are a number of scientific and political objections to this approach. In the first place, we can only investigate racial differences if we can first define what race is and then carry out appropriate studies. As Jones (1991) points out, there are a number of problems including:

- the difficulty in defining race;
- the history of social movement that has meant that many people have ancestors from many parts of the world;
- within-race variability is much greater than between-race variability (see above);
- when comparative research is carried out, it has so far been impossible to obtain comparable samples of people from different races.

The idea that there are biologically different races of people is controversial to say the least. The only way that race can be effectively defined is geographically or politically; in which case we are defining people by social criteria and not biological ones, and the differences are most likely to be due to social differences such as income and opportunity. (Note: this issue of perceived racial differences is also briefly discussed in Chapter 5, on psychometrics.)

Despite the obvious theoretical, practical and political problems with writing about race differences, the premier journal of the British Psychological Society chose to publish the article by Rushton (1990) which put forward an academically shallow but openly racist set of ideas. To give you a flavour of the article, I include part of the 'table of results' (see Table 4.1). I have some concerns about including something like this because it is very offensive, but I hope it also appears quite ridiculous. I have not changed any part of these items from the original table of results.

The first major problem with the article is the division of the world's people into three races. The justification for this is slight if not non-existent. Then if we look at the table we see differences expressed in very general terms. Life span is assessed as highest in 'mongoloids' and lowest in 'negroids'. The most likely explanation for this are the famines that have plagued Africa for much of the twentieth century. Another item in the table suggests that the age of first intercourse is 'slow' in 'mongoloids'. This seems a strange item to have in the table for two reasons, first because it does not seem to make sense (what does it mean to have a 'slow age of first intercourse'?), and secondly

Table 4.1 Part of the bizarre 'table of results' from Rushton's article

	Mongoloids	Caucasoids	Negroids
"Excess neurons"	8.90 m	8.65 m	8.55 m
Age of walking	slow	medium	fast
Age of first intercourse	slow	medium	fast
Age of first pregnancy	slow	medium	fast
Life span	long	medium	short
Aggressiveness	low	medium	high
Sociability	low	medium	high
Law abidance	high	medium	low
Mental health	high	medium	low

Source: Rushton (1990)

because it appears to be a pointless observation. It is there, however, because of the underlying theoretical idea behind the work, that is the idea of **neoteny**.

Neoteny is the extension in childhood that evolution has given human beings. Most animals are born with their brains fully formed or fairly nearly formed. The chimpanzee has the greatest post-birth development, but that stops after nine months. Human brains, however, continue to develop until we are about twenty years old. This is what gives us our adaptability. The argument that Rushton made was that some races have a longer childhood than others and are, therefore, further down the evolutionary road. The attempt to argue that one race is biologically superior to another is not new. Since Darwin first made suggestions along these lines, people have tried to find scientific justifications for the exploitation of one group of people by another. The scientific arguments do not stand up to scrutiny, though this has not stopped their popularisation.

The argument by Rushton is an example of *scientific racism*, which we define as the attempt to justify racial politics through the use of bogus scientific arguments. This is not unique to Rushton, or indeed to psychology. What is most remarkable about this story is not that some people put forward racist views attached to bogus science, but that a prestigious journal should choose to publish it.

The study of prejudice

Prejudice has been of particular interest to social psychologists. Many textbooks carry discussions of it, and some of the studies are among the most well known of psychological investigations and theories. Among the important studies are the work of Adorno *et al.* (1950) on the authoritarian personality, the work of Sherif (1956) on the conflict theory of prejudice, and the work of Tajfel (1970) on minimal groups. One feature that united all this work was that it looked at the

Look back at the definition of ethnocentrism.

- What groups do you feel part of? (for example, family, football fan, etc.)
- What groups do you feel excluded from?
- Think of some examples of your own ethnocentrism.

Progress exercise

person who is prejudiced and tried to explain their behaviour. This was obviously of great interest, but there was a missing voice here, that of the victim of prejudice. For every act of prejudice, there is the person who acts out the prejudice and the person who is the object of that action. It is further example of the implicit racism of psychology that we largely study racists (predominantly White people in the USA and Britain) and ignore the victims of racism.

Women and science

As we saw above, science has been used to justify a number of racist beliefs. It has also been used to justify a number of sexist ones. There was a prevailing belief in nineteenth-century science that women were inferior to men. For example, Darwin wrote:

The chief distinction in the intellectual powers of the two sexes is shown by man's attaining to a higher eminence, in whatever he takes up, than can woman – whether requiring deep thought, reason, or imagination, or merely the use of the senses and hands.

(Darwin, cited in Shields, 1978, p. 752)

One of the 'findings' of this period came from the pioneering physiological psychologist Broca, who studied the relative sizes of people's brains. He concluded that on average, women have smaller brains than men, and that this meant they were less intelligent than men. As Gould (1978) pointed out, however, the averages were not adjusted to take account of height (taller people have bigger brains), or age (older people are more likely to have reduced brain size). The women in Broca's sample were smaller and older than the men, and these factors explain the difference in the average size of the brains studied by Broca.

Another argument that was common at the turn of the twentieth century, and still raises its little head from time to time, is the **variability hypothesis**. Put simply, this suggests that the range of scores for men on a number of psychological measures is wider than the range of scores for women. This means, for example, that we expect to see more very stupid men than very stupid women, but we also expect to see more very clever men than very clever women. Those of you who have been out at Whitley Bay on a Friday night will have seen considerable evidence for the first suggestion, but there is very little evidence to support the second suggestion. The idea behind the variability hypothesis is that the reason for the high proportion of men in powerful positions is because there are more gifted men than there are women, and that they do not owe their positions to any social variables but to their perceived greater abilities. It is possible to make a robust challenge to the variability hypothesis, but as Shields (1978) argues, the scientific argument that is accepted is the one that often conforms to the social beliefs of that time and that culture.

Sexism in psychology

Women have had a difficult job being recognised in psychology. The content of psychology has largely been concerned with male behaviour and male experience, and academic psychology has created a number of barriers to the development and acceptance of its female colleagues.

Women psychologists do not make a prominent appearance in the written histories of psychology (Furumoto and Scarborough, 1992). This is despite the fact that they made a significant contribution to the development of the subject. In 1906 Cattell published the first edition of *American Men of Science* (dodgy title or what?), which contained 4,000 entries. Even though psychology was still a very new science, the list contained 186 psychologists, of whom 22 were women. This achievement was all the more remarkable since up to the turn of the twentieth century, most of the major American universities would not allow women to take graduate degrees in psychology. Furumoto and Scarborough (1992) compared the careers of these women with their male colleagues and found that they were less likely to achieve the same professional status, and those that did were all unmarried. They went on to note that a number of gender-specific factors affected the experience of these women psychologists including (a) exclusion from certain positions because they were women, (b) having the responsibility for other members of their families that is not expected of men, and (c) a dilemma between marriage and developing a career.

How psychology deals with women

In the content of psychology, there has been an pervasive belittlement of women. If you look at the following quotes from famous male psychologists you will start to get the picture:

> We must start with the realisation that, as much as women want to be good scientists or engineers, they want first and foremost to be womanly companions of men and to be mothers.
>
> (Bruno Bettelheim, 1965, cited in Weisstein, 1992, p. 61)

> Much of a young woman's identity is already defined in her kind of attractiveness and in the selectivity of her search for the man (or men) by whom she wishes to be sought...
>
> (Erik Erikson, 1964, cited in Weisstein, 1992, p. 62)

> Nor will you have escaped worrying about this problem – those of you who are men; to those of you who are women this will not apply – you are yourself the problem.
>
> (Sigmund Freud, 1973, p. 146. These lectures were first published in 1933.)

These quotes all show a very male view of women. Many men have these views, but it is important to distinguish between personal views and scientific descriptions of behaviour and experience. What makes the above so damaging is that they pretend to be something more than the prejudiced views of bar room critics. Even more disturbing is the quote from psychiatrist Antony Storr, below:

> The idea of being seized and borne off by a ruthless male who will wreak his sexual will upon his helpless victim has a universal appeal to the female sex.
>
> (Storr, 1968, p. 91)

The idea that women want to be raped by violent men might have universal appeal to men but it surely has no appeal to women. It is frightening to see male violence legitimised by psychology in this way.

The above quotes are just a selection from a large sample of possible contributions. Women have largely been dealt with by psychology either as a problem, or as the nurturers of children and men. It is fair to say that women's voices are now louder in psychology than they were, but the body of knowledge that is used as psychological evidence still requires an analysis that highlights its gender bias.

It is worth noting how many of the classic studies in psychology were largely carried out on male subjects. For example, two of the most cited studies on prejudice, Sherif's (1956) study of conflict and competition, and Tajfel's (1970) minimal group studies were both carried out on boys. Kitzinger (1998) also points out that Erikson's model of identity across the life span is based on interviews with males, and Kohlberg's theory of moral development is based on a series of studies and interviews with males.

Feminist psychology

Feminist psychology starts from two basic assumptions (Kitzinger, 1998):

- women are worthwhile human beings and worthy of study in their own right
- social change is needed to improve women's situation

The first point is a basic statement about human dignity and many people would buy into this without much hesitation (or at least pay lip service to it). The second point is more controversial since it positions psychology as an agent of social change. This goes against the scientific notion that psychology should be objective and detached rather than involved and active. However, other parts of this text describe how psychology has been active in the furtherance of warfare and propaganda, so it is not plausible to argue that it should stand outside the debate for political and social change.

The psychology that has excluded women in the past has also led to an inadequate understanding of men, because it has failed to acknowledge the particular features of being male that structure their lives (Kitzinger, 1998). As a result, men and masculinity are also a key topic in feminist psychology. Other topics include false memory syndrome and child sexual abuse, anorexia and eating disorders, rape, menstruation and sexual negotiation. Kitzinger (1998) argues that feminist perspectives in psychology have gone beyond challenging gender bias and have added a new dimension to psychology. This dimension asks questions about the lives of ordinary people, their relationships and how they can be enabled to contribute more to a wide range of human activities.

Psychologists such as Carol Tavris have taken another look at some psychological findings and put a different interpretations on them. For example, Tavris (1991) noted that the following conclusions have been drawn from research into sex differences:

- women have lower self-esteem than men;
- women do not value their efforts as much as do men, even when they are doing the same work;
- women are more likely to say they are hurt than to admit they are angry;
- women have more difficulty than men in developing a separate sense of self,

Tavris noted that these findings are all phrased to emphasise the perceived problems of women. It is possible, however, to describe the same findings in a different way that emphasises the problems of men. Look at the following, compare them with the above list and see which you think is the better description:

- men are more conceited than women;
- men overvalue the work they do;
- men are more likely to accuse and attack others when they are unhappy, rather than describing their hurt and asking for sympathy and support;
- men have more difficulty than women in forming and maintaining attachments.

It's not that one set of statements is right and the other is wrong, it is that each contains a degree of bias and interpretation. Tavris suggested that this bias usually describes the perceived problems of women rather than the perceived problems of men.

More examples of bias in psychology

The next section of this chapter looks at some examples of bias in psychology. This is not meant to be a comprehensive list but to give a flavour of the biases that exist, and to suggest how you might read psychology with an eye to any underlying bias. Some further discussion of bias in psychology can be found in the introduction to this text, and also in Chapter 5 on psychometrics.

Cross-cultural studies

Psychology has a tradition of looking at people from a range of cultures. This work is often referred to as cross-cultural studies. Although it provides a wider picture of human behaviour and experience than can be gained by just looking at our own culture, there are some problems with this approach, especially as it is presented in textbooks. The people from cultures other than our own are sometimes presented as quite exotic – strange people from strange countries doing strange things. They are often described in a way that compares them against some idea of a Western norm. An example of this is the study on perception by Turnbull (1961) which is commonly cited in textbooks where the subjects are referred to as pygmies, and characterised as primitive and superstitious.

One of the issues to consider is the language we use to describe people and their behaviour. We might say that someone belongs to a group, or a culture or a nation or a tribe. Each of these terms carries a number of assumptions with it. It is hard to imagine a context where we would describe someone from Yorkshire as belonging to a tribe, but we might use that term to describe someone from Africa. Our selective use of these terms probably shows our ethnocentric attitudes towards certain groups of people. Howitt (1991) gives an example of this from the introductory text by Atkinson *et al.* (1990) – (the emphasis is added by Howitt):

> Behaviour that is considered normal by one society may be considered abnormal by another. For example, members of some African *tribes* do not consider it unusual to hear voices when no one is actually talking or to see visions when nothing is actually there, but such behaviours are considered abnormal in most *societies*.
>
> (Atkinson *et al.*, 1990, page 592)

So, according to Atkinson *et al.*, Africans live in tribes, whereas other people live in societies. Who else lives in tribes?

> In another chimpanzee border war observed during the 1970s, a *tribe* of about 15 chimpanzees destroyed a smaller neighbouring group by killing the members off one male at a time.
>
> (Atkinson *et al.*, 1990, page 427)

If we use the term 'tribe' to describe animal behaviour, it suggests that we see that behaviour as being less sophisticated that the behaviour we see in a 'culture'. The fact that texts use the term casually to describe African peoples implies there is a negative attitude towards these people.

It is worth noting that the patronising approach to cross cultural studies approach is declining, and there are now a number of texts available that deal with psychological issues from a broader perspective than we are used to reading. These texts include Smith and Bond (1993), Azibo (1996), Matsumoto (1994) and Moghaddam *et al.* (1993).

Moral development

One of the most influential pieces of work in this area is the research of Kohlberg. He identified three levels of morality each sub-divided into two stages, and suggested that the stages map on to cognitive development (Kohlberg, 1968). According to Kohlberg, at the first level (the pre-conventional level) the child responds to other people's definitions of good and bad behaviour. At the second level (the conventional level), the child internalises the rules of his or her society, and judges good and bad in terms of social approval and respect for authority. At the most developed third level (the post-conventional level), the child develops a number of abstract and ethical values that they use to judge situations and events.

There are two main criticisms of this approach that suggest it contains ethnocentric bias:

(a) Carol Gilligan (for example, Gilligan and Attanucci, 1988) suggested that male values are given a higher status than female values in Kohlberg's theory. The idea that values can be individual and abstract and free from a concern for the effects on people is a male outlook. She suggested that men are concerned with abstract notions of justice guided by rational principles, and by fairness. Women, on the other hand, see things in concrete social terms, taking into account compassion, caring, human relationships and special responsibilities to family, friends, associates, and so on. She proposed, therefore, that women's moral development is qualitatively different to that of men's.

(b) Kohlberg's (1968) own work on cross-cultural aspects of his theory found that according to his scale, Americans were more morally advanced than any other nationality. According to these studies the average Turkish sixteen-year-old, for example, has a similar moral understanding to the average ten-year-old American. The most likely explanations for this discrepancy are not that Americans are morally superior to Turkish people, but that (a) the theory of moral development only applies to Americans, or (b) the tests for moral development do not apply to all cultures.

Concepts of self

In Western culture, and therefore also Western psychology, we have an idea that people are separate individuals who stand completely alone. In psychology we talk about the self-concept which refers to the way I perceive myself as being quite unique, unconnected to any other person. This philosophy of the self is not held by all cultures. A powerful critique of this approach was provided by Nobles (1976). Nobles identified two important themes in European/American science:

(a) survival of the fittest
(b) control over nature

Our explanations of the world are still influenced by Darwin's ideas about natural selection, and much of our technology is aimed towards overcoming the environment we live in. This usually means covering it with concrete. Nobles suggested that these themes are reflected in the European/American emphasis on competition, individual rights, independence and separateness. In psychology this has led to an emphasis on individuality, uniqueness and individual differences.

By contrast, the themes of the African world view, according to Nobles, are

(a) survival of the people
(b) oneness with nature

The contrast with Western values could not be greater. The group are more important than the individual, and the environment is there to be adjusted to rather than changed. These themes are reflected in the African values of cooperation, interdependence and collective responsibility. The psychological emphasis would then be on commonality, groupness and similarity. The differences in the two approaches are summarised in Figure 4.3.

Nobles argued that in understanding the traditional African concept of self we must consider the belief that 'I am because We are, and because We are therefore I am.' A person's self-definition is dependent on the definition of the people. Therefore, if we try and describe all people using the Western ideas about self concept, we will fail to see the social links and understandings of many people in cultures other than those of America and Europe.

Psychology and culture

The study of cultural difference goes beyond the scope of this text, but it is possible here to give a brief taste of the importance of this work and to show how it helps us further understand human behaviour and experience. Psychologists working in countries outside America and Europe have found that the methods and theories of American and European psychology do not address the issues that are most important to them. Smith and Bond (1993) described how social psychologists in these countries have become less interested in describing and analysing what is happening (the status quo) and more concerned with trying to initiate positive social changes. This has an interesting parallel with the approach of feminist psychology described above.

When we consider the value of American and European psychology, it is worth looking at how well the famous studies can be replicated in other countries. In the final section of this chapter, we will have a brief look at the social psychology of social loafing, conformity and obedience. For a more extended review of these replications, see Smith and Bond (1993).

Social loafing

Social loafing refers to the situation where several people are carrying out the same task and each individual may feel they do not need to put in the maximum effort. In other words, in group activities people do not pull their weight. For example, Latané *et al.* (1979) looked at how loudly people shouted or clapped in groups of different sizes compared to when they were alone, and found that the average output is less in groups. This is a fairly robust finding on a range of activities, though it has also been found that social loafing declines when the activity is important and when the individuals believe they are being monitored by the other people in the group.

Social loafing is not a universal behaviour pattern, however, and studies have found that the reverse can occur in other cultures. For example, Earley (1989) compared the behaviour of Chinese and

American managers in their approach to desk work. They were asked to carry out a number of tasks and given a clear target of how many to complete in one hour. Some were asked to work alone and complete twenty tasks. The others were asked to work in groups of ten and the group was expected to complete 200 tasks. Clearly, if all the managers pulled their weight in the group they would still complete twenty tasks. The results showed that, in the groups, the Americans tended to complete less than twenty tasks (showing signs of social loafing) whereas the Chinese completed more than twenty tasks. It would appear that group membership and social responsibility have a different value in China to what they have in America.

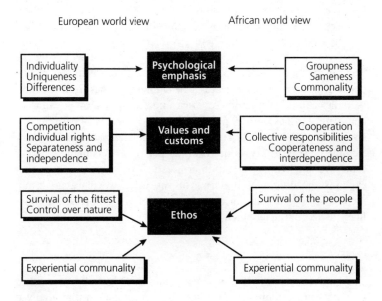

Figure 4.3 **African and European world views**

Source: Nobles (1976, p. 20)

Conformity

The study that first comes to mind in discussions on conformity is the work of Asch (1955) which showed that when people are asked to make a simple perceptual judgement in the presence of a group of people who all disagree with them, about one-third will go along with the judgment of the majority. At least, this is how it is usually presented. Another way of putting it would be to say how two-thirds of the people resist the majority and express their independence. It is an interesting observation that American psychology has chosen to see this study as an example of conformity rather than an example of independence.

There have been numerous replications of the Asch studies in America and also in many other countries including Brazil, Hong Kong, Zimbabwe and Fiji. Smith and Bond (1993) presented the data from thirty of these studies and compared the results from 'collectivist' and 'individualist' countries. By 'collectivist', they mean cultures that value group activity and achievement above individual activity and achievement. These are clearly very broad terms and there will be a lot of variation within a culture, but if we accept the general distinction it is possible to see a difference in the results between the two sets of cultures. The eighteen studies from the individualist countries (mainly America and Europe) show a range of conformity values from 39 per cent down to as low as 14 per cent. On the other hand, the twelve studies from the collectivist countries show a range of conformity values from 25 per cent to as high as 58 per cent. We might suggest an interpretation of these findings that explains the difference in terms of the value we place on group membership. If it is important to be part of the group we are more likely to accept the judgment of the group.

Obedience

The Milgram study (1963), where a member of the public was asked to carry out a training programme on another person that involved giving them potentially fatal electric shocks, is perhaps the most famous and most provocative study in social psychology. Variations of this study have been conducted in many countries obtaining a range of results. Smith and Bond (1993) produced a review of twelve of these studies and found a fair degree of cultural variation in obedience, ranging from 92 per cent obedience to only 12 per cent obedience. Smith and Bond offered two conclusions from their review: first, substantial numbers of people from a variety of countries will harm other people on the instructions of an authority figure; and second, levels of obedience vary a lot, and this variation depends on the social context of the study and the meaning of the orders that are given by the authority figure. This second point suggests that we are not blindly obedient to authority as is often suggested, but that we respond to the social and physical context in which we receive the orders.

Summary

The above examples illustrate how important it is to look at again at the findings of psychology (by which I mean American and European psychology), and see whether those findings can be repeated in other cultures. The benefits of this approach are:

(a) a better understanding of the concepts that are applied to American and European people; and
(b) an appreciation of the experience and behaviour of other peoples.

I said in the introduction to this text that I cannot pretend to be objective, that is, free from bias. I obviously have a number of biases and they come out to a greater or lesser extent in this text. You might like to consider:

- What are the biases of the author?
- What groups does he belong to?
- What newspaper does he read?

Review exercise

Further reading

Matsumoto, D. (1994) *People: Psychology from a Cultural Perspective*, California: Brooks/Cole. An introductory test that covers many of the key areas of psychology and considers the issues surrounding cultural diversity.

Moghaddam, F.M., Taylor, D.M. and Wright, S.C. (1993) *Social Psychology in Cross-Cultural Perspective*, New York: W.H. Freeman. An introductory test that covers many of the key areas of psychology and considers the issues surrounding cultural diversity.

Williams, J.H. (1987) *Psychology of Women*, 3rd edn, New York: Norton. Many psychology texts cover this subject using a very neutral, at best, or male agenda. This text adds a bit of balance to the debate.

Psychometric testing

Introduction

Psychometric testing produces some of the greatest differences of opinion and some of the strongest arguments to be found in psychology. The arguments often get confused because of the mixture of scientific and political issues that come into play. There are arguments about:

- practical issues: do the tests give accurate and consistent results? Do the complex statistical procedures illuminate or disguise what is going on?
- theoretical issues: do the tests measure underlying psychological qualities? For example, is there such a quality as 'intelligence' and is it measured by an IQ test?
- political issues: can the tests be used to look at differences between groups of people, for example different social classes, or different

ethnic groups, or the differences between men and women? What are the social and political consequences of using tests to categorise people?

In this chapter we will look at all these main issues, though it must be said that some of the arguments are quite complex and cannot be argued in full in the space that is available. The chapter starts with a brief review of the technology of psychometric testing which has been developing for over 100 years. We will then look at intelligence testing and its rather dubious past, and finally we will take a brief look at some issues in personality testing.

The technology of psychometric tests

The term 'psychometric' means 'measuring the mind', though many psychometricians would be very uncomfortable with a term such as 'mind'. A psychological test is a task or set of tasks that can be given in a standard format to an individual, and which produce a score that can be represented as a number (or a category). It can involve almost any activity. Most commonly, for reasons of practicality, it involves filling in a questionnaire. Tests are used to measure cognitive functions (for example, IQ tests), personality (for example, Eysenck's EPI, see below), mood (for example, the Beck Depression Inventory), attitudes (for example, political opinion polls), aptitude for various jobs (for example, the Comprehensive Ability Battery), illness behaviour (for example, the McGill Pain Inventory), and many other qualities. Psychometric tests are extensively used in everyday life, and you are likely to come into contact with them on a fairly regular basis.

Performance and ability

One of the first issues to consider is the distinction between **performance** and **ability**. Performance is what you actually do, and ability is what you are capable of. It is a common experience of students that their teachers say 'you have the ability, but you are not doing the work'. They mean that the reason you got a Grade E in your examinations was due to poor performance and not poor ability (and obviously not the teacher's fault either). Any test we give to someone can only measure their performance on that test, and not their ability.

We can only infer their ability from that performance. So when we are measuring intelligence, we are, in fact, measuring *performance* on the particular test and not the underlying *intellectual ability*.

The problem that arises when we interpret the results of a test is the many factors that affect performance. These factors include:

- language of the test: words mean different things to different people, and performance can be affected by our level of understanding of the questions.
- test situation: some people work well in quiet environments with few distractions, whereas others can only concentrate if the television is on in the background.
- expectations: if you expect that you will not be able to answer the questions you will be more likely to give up easily.
- motivation: if you are competitive and want to win everything then you will try harder to do well (if it is an IQ test, for example)

Measuring people

To measure something you have to compare it against something else. If we are measuring a table, it is easy because we can use a ruler, but if we are measuring people what can we use? There are three ways in which we can use tests to measure people:

1   direct measurement: where we use a physical measure such as grip strength or reaction time. Although these measures can be useful, there are only a limited number of direct measures we can make of people.
2   criterion-referenced measurement: where we compare the performance of an individual against an ideal performance.
3   norm-referenced measurement: where we compare the performance of an individual against performance of other people, most commonly the peer group. This is far and away the most common way of using psychological tests.

An example of norm-referenced measurement can be seen in IQ testing. As children get older, they develop their educational skills and so get more answers correct on an IQ test. This is not taken to mean that their IQ is improving, even though their intellectual skills are improving. The individual is compared against children of the same age, so their IQ score represents their ranking in their own age group. This measure has a number of benefits in that it tells you how well you are doing compared to people like you. It also, however, gives a lot of emphasis to the differences between individuals, even when those differences might be very small.

Test reliability

If we are using a psychometric test, we need to know whether it will give us a consistent result. So, if we give someone the test on a Wednesday afternoon, we hope to get the same results as if we had given the test on Friday morning. It would remarkable if we got exactly the same result because all forms of measurement have an element of error in them, but we hope this error is relatively small. Psychologists use a number of techniques for assessing **reliability** including:

1   Test–retest: in this case we administer the test on two occasions and compare the scores using a correlation technique. Test–retest reliability is affected by a number of factors including:

  (i)   changes in subjects: for example if we leave a gap of three months between the test and re-test of an IQ test we can reasonably expect children to develop their intellectual skills in that time, and since children develop at different rates, their rank order will also change during that time. This will reduce the test–retest reliability calculation.

  (ii) measurement error: for example, changes in mood brought about by a hangover for one administration of the test, poor test instructions so the subjects do not grasp what is required, and guessing, which people always do but produces a degree of unreliability in the scores.

  (iii) other factors: for example, if the time gap between the two test times is very brief then the subjects are likely to remember their answers, or if the questions are very easy, then you will get a high reliability value because the subjects get them nearly all right on both occasions.

2   Internal consistency reliability: in this case, we compare two parts
     of the test to see how similar the scores are.

Before the arrival of desktop computers, the most common way to
calculate internal consistency was through split-half reliability. This
method correlates the response to half the items (for example, the
odd-numbered items) to the other items (the even-numbered items).
This gives a rough approximation of the reliability value, although a
number of corrections are made to the scores to take account of such
things as test length (the longer the test the greater the reliability, so if
you split the test into two you inevitably reduce the reliability score).

A more sophisticated version of the split-halves technique looks at
all the possible split halves and gives a value of reliability called
Coefficient Alpha. This makes an estimate of the amount of error in
the test and hence what the 'true' score would be without any error. It
then compares your score with this 'true' score to give a measure of
reliability.

All of the above reliability techniques have serious errors because
they make assumptions about the data that are rarely appropriate
(Shevlin, 1995, 1998). Psychometricians, therefore, use more complex
measures of reliability that use a similar principle to that used by Coefficient Alpha but do not make so many assumptions of the data.

The above is an incredibly brief summary of the statistical procedures surrounding reliability, but believe me, you do not want to see
the full details or the mathematical formulae. I can already sense
many reader's eyelids becoming more heavy as they work their way
through this section. (Note: if you are interested in the technology of
testing, then you should refer to Kline, 1993, or Kaplan and Saccuzzo,
1993, and then seek help from your general practitioner or personal
counsellor).

We can take two general points from the above. First, there are a
number of statistical controversies in psychometrics about how to
evaluate the data. Second, we can see that measurement always
contains error, but psychologists have been developing statistical tools
for over one hundred years to reduce this error, and the whole testing
business is statistically very sophisticated. As a result, there are a
number of reliable psychometric tests that are used to measure a wide
range of psychological variables.

Test validity

A test is said to be valid if it measures what it claims to measure. So we consider whether a depression scale measures depression, and whether an IQ test measures intelligence. This is not as obvious as it sounds, and it is a complex process to measure this validity.

There are a number of types of validity, but perhaps the most important is construct validity. If a test has construct validity it matches up with a psychological concept or theory. If a test has construct validity then the following should occur:

- the scores of the test should correlate with other tests of the same psychological quality.
- the scores of the test should not correlate with tests of different psychological qualities.
- the scores of the test should predict future performance.
- the test items should have some connection to the appropriate psychological theory.

All this is easier said than done, and psychometricians go to great lengths to establish the validity of their tests. Many of these tests, however, continue to attract controversy about what they actually measure.

Standardisation

The idea of standardisation rests on the principle that abilities, both mental and physical, are distributed throughout a population according to a normal distribution curve. This curve describes a set of scores where a few people obtain extreme high scores, a few people obtain extreme low scores, and most people score around the average. If we assume the scores are normally distributed then we can make judgments about the performance of an individual using the statistics of standard deviation and z-scores.

Standardising a test involves establishing how the scores of this test are distributed among the population, and making sure that the test, if administered to enough people, will produce a normal distribution. This involves testing large numbers of people and establishing what the normal scores for those types of people might be. From this, it is possible to develop population norms, which identify what would be an average score, what would be above-average, and what would be below-average; so standardisation, at least in theory, allows us to judge how typical, or uncommon, someone's result is.

The major issues here concern first, the selection of samples for the standardisation procedure, and second, the assumption that the scores are normally distributed. If we wanted to know the average IQ score of the people in this country, we could give everyone a test and work out the mean score. This is clearly impracticable, so we select a sample from the whole population and use the results of that sample to estimate the average score of the populations. Clearly there will be some error in this estimate, but the amount of error will depend on how representative our sample is.

Summary

The above brief discussion of the technology of psychological tests gives a flavour of the sophistication of test construction and the practical problems involved in constructing and interpreting tests. The controversies are mainly of a technical nature and concern the potential error in tests and how predictive they can be of future behaviour. The arguments might appear a little remote and technical, but without some understanding of the technicalities it is not possible to argue about the other issues that arise out of psychological testing. For example, it was the failure of psychologists to consider scientifically the data offered by British psychologist Cyril Burt that allowed him to get away with scientific fraud on the topic of intelligence testing (see Hearnshaw, 1979).

Testing intelligence

The testing of intelligence is perhaps the single most controversial issue in psychology. In the space available, I can only touch on a few of the issues and try and give you some idea of the strength of feeling that this topic produces. The following two quotes give some idea of the spread of opinion on this topic.

NEW FROM SCOOBY ENTERPRISES
(The Company that Measures the Mind)

THE PSYCHOMEASURE INTELLIGENCE TEST

For only £25.00 (plus P & P) you can have the equipment to measure the intelligence of your friends, employees, teachers etc.

Easy to use and quick to analyse the PSYCHOMEASURE offers the ideal alternative to time consuming I.Q. tests. All you have to do is to place the PSYCHOMEASURE around the forehead of the subject and read off the intelligence score.

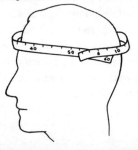

Figure 5.1 The Psycho-Scooby measure of intelligence

1 Which of the following statements best describes the PSYCHOMEASURE INTELLIGENCE TEST:

   a The test is reliable and valid
   b The test is reliable but not valid
   c The test is valid but not reliable
   d The test is neither reliable nor valid

2 Describe one way that you could assess the reliability of the PSYCHOMEASURE test.

3 Describe one way that you could assess the validity of the PSYCHOMEASURE test.

4 Most IQ tests have a bias in them that gives certain people better scores than others. Describe ONE bias in the PSYCHOMEASURE INTELLIGENCE TEST.

The measurement of intelligence is psychology's most telling accomplishment to date.

(Herrnstein, 1973)

The IQ test has served as an instrument of oppression against the poor.

(Kamin, 1977)

The early tests

The earliest psychometric testing is usually attributed to Francis Galton who set up a stall at the International Health Exhibition in London in 1884 and tested visitors mental abilities for the sum of threepence (see Figure 5.2). As many as 9,000 people took the tests, which included measures of reaction times to sounds, lights and touch, and other easily measurable motor activities and sensory judgements. I mention Galton in particular because of his belief that intellectual abilities were inherited and his enthusiastic support of eugenic solutions to the problems of society. Eugenics refers to the attempt to improve the quality of human beings through selective breeding; so for example, if we wanted to improve the general level of intelligence in the country, we would encourage intelligent people to have lots of children and unintelligent people to have none. Ideas like this can have damaging social consequences, so it is important to challenge them.

There are many problems with the eugenics approach to intelligence including the assumptions that:

- there is a human quality that we can call intelligence; this may appear self evident, but it is possible to argue that we have many different types of intelligent behaviour rather than just one.
- intelligence can be reliably and validly measured; though as we have already seen (see above), the issues of reliability and validity remain controversial to this day.
- intelligence is a fixed quantity and cannot be improved; though it might be that intelligence can be improved through coaching.
- the differences in intelligence between people are mainly due to genetic factors; most controversial of all the assumptions, it also has the least scientific evidence to support it.

ANTHROPOMETRIC
LABORATORY

For the measurement in various ways of Human Form and Faculty.

Entered from the Science Collection of the S. Kensington Museum.

This laboratory is established by Mr. Francis Galton for the following purposes:—

1. For the use of those who desire to be accurately measured in many ways, either to obtain timely warning of remediable faults in development, or to learn their powers.

2. For keeping a methodical register of the principal measurements of each person, of which he may at any future time obtain a copy under reasonable restrictions. His initials and date of birth will be entered in the register, but not his name. The names are indexed in a separate book.

3. For supplying information on the methods, practice, and uses of human measurement.

4. For anthropometric experiment and research, and for obtaining data for statistical discussion.

Charges for making the principal measurements:
THREEPENCE each, to those who are already on the Register.
FOURPENCE each, to those who are not:— one page of the Register will thenceforward be assigned to them, and a few extra measurements will be made, chiefly for future identification.

The Superintendent is charged with the control of the laboratory and with determining in each case, which, if any, of the extra measurements may be made, and under what conditions.

H. & W. Brown, Printers, 20 Fulham Road, S.W.

Figure 5.2 Advertisement for Galton's early tests

All these assumptions are controversial and we will consider them further below. The important issue to bear in mind at this point is that intelligence testing has been consistently linked with genetic explanations of individual differences, and with scientists who proposed genetic solutions to social problems.

Binet's pioneering tests

The first tests that we can recognise as IQ tests were developed in France by Alfred Binet, who started his scientific studies by examining the relationship between head size and intelligence. He discovered that there was little connection between size of head and intelligence. He was later commissioned by the Minister of Public Education to develop a technique to identify children in need of special education, and from this the intelligence test was born. The test was used to give an estimate of a child's mental age by comparing the child's performance on various tasks with the performance of children of various ages. It was later suggested that the mental age of the child should be divided by the chronological age to give an index of intelligence, and so the notion of IQ was developed (the formula is given below). This is an example of norm referencing (see above).

Intelligence Quotient (IQ) = Mental Age/Chronological Age $\times$ 100

Binet believed that children who were in need of extra help could be identified by these tests, but he vigorously argued against the idea that intelligence is a fixed quantity that cannot be improved by further help. This approach got sadly lost in the translation of tests into the English and in their transportation to America. In contrast to the approach of Binet, the fiercest supporters of intelligence testing in the English-speaking world were scientists who believed that individual differences are mainly due to genetic factors, and who proposed eugenic solutions to the perceived problems of society. For example, Lewis Terman, who introduced the IQ test to America while he was professor of psychology at Stanford University, wrote:

> If we would preserve our state for a class of people worthy to possess it, we must prevent, as far as possible, the propagation of mental degenerates.
>
> (Lewis Terman, 1921, cited in Kamin, 1977)

The big words disguise the sentiments of the quote. To paraphrase Terman, he is saying we must stop poor and uneducated people from having children. All this would seem unpleasant but unimportant, were it not for that fact that over half of the states in the USA brought in sterilisation laws for the 'feeble minded' and carried out tens of thousands of operations (Kamin, 1977).

The first mass IQ testing

American psychologist Robert Yerkes was concerned to establish psychology as a 'hard' science and thought that mental testing looked a promising route to achieve this. Unfortunately, in 1915 mental testing did not enjoy much credibility, so Yerkes tried to change this. The outbreak of the First World War (1914–18) in Europe and the subsequent involvement of the USA brought about a massive mobilisation of armies. Yerkes managed to persuade the American military to give mental tests to all army recruits, and as a result he was able to preside over the testing of 1.75 million recruits.

There were three types of test: literate recruits were given a written test called the Army Alpha, men who were illiterate or who failed the Alpha were given a pictorial test called the Army Beta, and failures on the Beta were to be recalled for an individual spoken examination. The Alpha had eight parts made up of the items we recognise today as IQ tests, such as analogies, filling in the missing number and unscrambling a sentence. The Beta test had seven parts including number work and the picture completion task shown in Figure 5.3. Each test took less than an hour and could be administered to large groups.

Yerkes asserted that the tests measured 'native intellectual ability' (cited in Gould, 1981, p. 349) but the level of cultural and educational knowledge required is illustrated in the examples given below.

- 'Washington is to Adams as first is to…'
- 'Crisco is a: patent medicine, disinfectant, toothpaste, food product'

Part six of examination Beta for testing innate intelligence.

Figure 5.3 **Some items from the pictorial part of Yerkes' mental tests**

Source: Gould (1984)

- 'Christy Mathewson is famous as a: writer, artist, baseball player, comedian.'

There were a number of problems in the administration of the tests. In particular, many who were illiterate in English were still allocated to the Alpha test and so scored zero or near to zero. This created a systematic bias in the test since recent immigrants who had a poor grasp of English, and Black men who had not been given much, if any, formal education were unable to score on the Alpha test. Another problem was that even the Beta test required the use of a pencil and the writing of numbers, and many men had never held a pencil in their lives.

The tests generated a lot of interest, and by 1921 when Yerkes published his findings he was able to refer to 'the steady stream of requests from commercial concerns, educational institutions and individuals for the use of army methods of psychological examining or for adaptation of such methods to special needs.' Mental testing and psychology had achieved the credibility that Yerkes wanted.

Gould (1981) reports that three 'facts' were created from the testing data;

1 The average mental age of white Americans was about 13. Unfortunately, this had been defined as the intellectual level of a moron, so the tests appeared to indicate that the average American was a moron. (Note: I advise readers to hold their ethnocentrism in check at this point.)
2 European immigrants could be graded by their country of origin.
3 The average score of Black men was lower than the average score of White men.

These three 'facts' can be adequately explained by the administration difficulties of the testing and the level of literacy of the groups of people taking the tests. In fact, a re-analysis of the data showed that performance depended on the length of time a person had lived in America, suggesting that culture and language played a large part in test performance. However, a much more sinister explanation was given for the results. It was argued that White people were superior to Black people, and that Americans were superior to many European peoples.

Once again, political beliefs triumphed over scientific analysis and the eugenic explanation took hold. One of the consequences of this was the passing of the Immigration Restriction Act in 1924 by the American Congress, which selectively stopped certain national groups from emigrating to the USA. The scientists who supported the eugenics argument lobbied the politicians and, according to Gould, 'won one of the greatest victories of scientific racism in American history.' (1981, p. 352)

Statistical techniques and intelligence testing

The need to interpret mental tests led to the development of a range of statistical techniques. Karl Pearson developed the correlation, and Charles Spearman developed factor analysis. Factor analysis has a particular importance in intelligence because it is used to suggest that there is such a thing as intelligence. This is not as obvious as it sounds. Just because we have a word for something, it does not mean that it exists. What we can observe is people behaving intelligently. but that does not mean they have a thing called intelligence.

If we give people a range of mental tests they do not do equally well on all of them. For example, people who are good at maths are not necessarily good at English or art. We could explain this by saying that these skills are entirely different, or we could say that there is an underlying skill of intelligence that affects our performance on all mental tests. The idea that intellectual differences are inherited depends on the simple idea that there is a single quality that affects performance. If there is no single quality of intelligence, then it clearly can not be inherited. This is the importance of the statistical analysis of test scores. If we can show there is a single intellectual quality then we can argue that intellectual differences are the result of genetic factors and we can suggest eugenic solutions. If, on the other hand, there is no single quality we can call intelligence, then the whole argument about inherited differences collapses.

It is important to note that Spearman, like many other intelligence testers of his time, favoured eugenic solutions and so was looking to establish that intelligence had a single characteristic. He developed the technique of factor analysis which analyses the relationship between a large number of correlations. He took the data from a range of mental tests and showed that there was one factor that explained the variations in scores on most of the tests. He called this factor 'g' (for general intelligence). This all looks very impressive and the complexity of the mathematics means that many people find it hard to argue against this finding. Gould (1981), however, provided a critique of Spearman's factor analysis of mental test data that challenges the existence of 'g' and therefore the existence of a underlying quality of intelligence. One of the arguments mounted by Gould is that you can use the same data to show the existence of several factors rather than just one.

The statistics, then, are not conclusive and the controversy remains about whether there is an underlying characteristic. Even if there is an underlying factor, it is by no means clear that we can call it intelligence. It could well be some cultural or environmental variable, for example, that affects our performance on all these tests.

Intelligence testing and race

As mentioned above, early IQ tests were used to suggest differences between different racial groups. This is an argument that has rumbled on for over 100 years without ever resolving itself. There are many problems with attempting any exploration of·racial differences (see Chapter 4 on bias in psychology), and none more so than the issue of intelligence. This is particularly controversial because differences between one group and another are often presented as differences in ability rather than differences in performance. In truth, the only evidence we have are performance scores, and we have to explain why groups perform differently. This could be due to a range of cultural, educational and motivational factors, and these explanations are much more plausible that any genetic explanations for the reasons described by Jones (see Chapter 4 of this text).

There is also the matter of how the genetic effect is calculated, and the statistic that is commonly cited is **heritability**. This statistic estimates how much the variation within any given population is due to genetic factors. It does not, however, tell us about why two populations will differ and so contributes nothing to our understanding of this issue (see Rose *et al.* 1984). It also fails to tell us anything about how much genetics affects the characteristics of an individual.

Problems like these make assertions about racial differences very difficult and, in fact, one of the leading psychometricians, Kline (1991) suggested that:

> The only advantage in setting out the different scores on IQ tests of racial groups is to give ammunition to those who wish to decry them. It adds nothing to theoretical understanding or to the social or educational practice.
>
> (Kline, 1991, p. 96)

IQ testing and expectation effects

One of the concerns about the use of psychometric tests, and IQ tests in particular, is that the results of the tests produce expectation effects. If, for example, an IQ test tells you that someone is a genius you might interpret their subsequent behaviour in terms of the test result and so expect them to behave in an intelligent way. It is fair to suggest that individuals may respond to the expectations of others, so if people expect you to be intelligent you are more likely to act intelligently.

In a famous but controversial study, Rosenthal and Jacobson (1968) set out to discover whether pupils' performance over the course of a school year could be affected simply by the expectations that their class teachers had of them. A proportion of children in an elementary school in the USA were labelled as 'bloomers'; that is they were identified to their class teachers as children who, on the basis of a psychological assessment, were expected to develop particularly rapidly in terms of intellect over the course of the following year. Unknown to the teachers, the bloomers had been chosen at random from each of the classes in the school. That is, there was actually no difference at the outset of the study between them and their classmates. If at the end of the year they had actually developed more rapidly than their classmates then this could be put down to the expectations that the teachers had of them. Presumably if pupils can perform better because of high expectations, the more worrying effect of pupils performing worse because of low expectations is also likely to be at work in everyday life.

The results appeared to support Rosenthal and Jacobson's hypothesis. However, there have been numerous criticisms of the study. For example, the IQ test they used was not standardised for the age-range of children on which it was used. Replication studies have found mixed results, and the effect described by Rosenthal and Jacobson is not as robust as they thought.

Rosenthal and Jacobson thought that one person's expectation of another person can become a more accurate prediction of their behaviour just because the expectation is there. The process behind this idea is more complex than it appears at first thought. The process of expectancy includes the following processes:

(i) teachers are assumed to have some expectations of their pupils, and that these expectations are based on some sort of evidence or hearsay;
(ii) these expectations affect the behaviour of the teacher in a visible way;
(iii) pupils perceive this 'communication' of the teacher's expectation;
(iv) the pupil's understanding of their teacher's expectations must affect their performance in class.

So the difficulty in replicating the study might be due to failure at any of these four stages. However, there has been some empirical support for the idea of these expectation effects and a good example of this is a quasi-experiment carried out by Seaver (1973). This study looked at teachers' expectations of children that were based on having already taught a sibling of the child. The question was whether teachers would expect the younger sibling to be like the elder child and whether this expectation would affect performance. Many of us have had the experience of being compared at school to a cleverer/better behaved/more responsible elder brother or sister. The teachers seem to have expectations of how we will behave based on their experience of our siblings. The study by Seaver confirmed this, and found that in classes where the teacher had experience of the elder sibling the student's results were more similar to their sibling's than they were in classes where the teacher had no knowledge of the sibling.

Summary

The testing of intelligence continues to generate a number of controversies including:

• whether there is such a thing as intelligence;

- whether we can accurately measure intelligence;
- how much genetic factors account for the differences in individual scores on IQ tests;
- how much genetic factors account for the differences in scores on IQ tests between groups of people;
- the political consequences of IQ data;
- the interpretation of complex statistical procedures;
- the effects of expectation on IQ performance;
- the problems of inferring intellectual ability from performance on IQ tests.

Measuring personality

Cattell and Butcher (1968) suggested there are three ways to approach the study of personality:

1 the literary approach in which the playwright or novelist describes people in a way that gives the reader an insight into human behaviour and experience;
2 clinical observation in which the clinician attempts to systematically classify normal and abnormal personalities;
3 the statistical tradition based on correlational methods and, in particular, factor analysis.

In this section, we will look at this third approach and consider some of the issues around measuring and quantifying personality characteristics. The measurement of personality does not create the same level of controversy as does the measurement of intelligence. The main reason for this is that the political impact of personality scores is not as great as IQ scores. Many of the same controversial issues, however, can be found in the measurement of both qualities, for example, the use of factor analysis, the validity of the tests, the issues surrounding the inheritance of personal qualities, and the historical connection between psychometric testing and eugenics.

Personality questionnaires

The popular way of measuring personality is through a questionnaire. The advantages are obvious in that questionnaires are relatively easy to construct, they are relatively easy to use with people, and it is relatively easy to establish norms. In short they are psychometrically efficient (Kline, 1993). The big problem to consider, however, is the one of validation. What do these reliable tests measure?

The problem comes with the use of factor analysis. When factor analysis is used to look at intellectual performance there is a theory that predicts how many factors there will be (in this case, one). In personality theory, however, the expected number of factors is by no means so obvious. Nobody would predict that all the differences between individuals can be explained by just one feature of personality, but how many are there? It is possible to come up with a number of factors just by the statistical method of factor analysis. Say, for example, that we put in the data from all our personality questionnaires and come up with four main factors that can be used to explain the data. The problem for the psychologists is to give these factors a name and show that they really exist. The alternative explanation is that the factors are just a trick of the numbers and have no existence outside the computer of a statistician.

Theories of personality

Factor analysis was used by Cattell to identify sixteen factors of personality, and he claimed that the 'sixteen personality-factor questionnaire' (16PF) measured the major factors of personality and could account for the differences between people. Cattell, therefore, discovered his sixteen factors through statistical means and the debate is about whether these are real factors that exist in people.

Another theory of personality that is also based on psychometric testing is that of H.J. Eysenck, in 1947, who described two major dimensions of personality: (i) introversion/extroversion, and (ii) neuroticism/stability. He argued that these are fundamental traits which account for a large proportion of individual differences. Eysenck's theory has generated a lot of research, possibly because it has two factors rather than sixteen.

Other researchers have identified different combinations of personality traits. McCrae and Costa (for example, 1985) suggested that there are five basic factors of personality, and there is now a weight of evidence that supports this view (Kline, 1993). These factors are derived from factor analysis, but the same factors appear in a

Table 5.1 The five robust factors		
1	Extroversion	Sometimes referred to in a slightly wider form as 'surgency'.
2	Emotional stability	Broader in scope that Eysenck's neuroticism, but essentially similar.
3	Agreeableness	Including traits of generosity, friendliness and interpersonal criticism
4	Control	Including traits of disorganisation, meticulous approaches to work, etc.
5	Culture	Including the traits of curiosity, creativity, intelligence and knowledgability.
Source: McCrae and Costa (1985, p. 716)		

range of studies giving support to the argument that the factors represent real psychological variables rather than just a statistical mirage. The five factors are shown in Table 5.1.

Expectation and the Barnum Effect

A serious problem with the Eysenck Personality Inventory (EPI), and also with similar tests, is to do with the expectation of the people taking the tests. Furnham and Varian (1988) looked at how people predict and accept their own test scores. In their first study, they asked undergraduates to try and predict their own and a well-known other person's personality scores on the EPI. They were fairly good at this. Then, in a second study, they gave some undergraduates false feedback about their scores after they had completed the EPI. The undergraduates were more likely to accept positive feedback (for example, 'you are a warm and considerate person') as accurate than negative feedback (for example, 'you are a miserable, smelly moron'), even though it did not have any connection with their actual scores.

This leads us to an inevitable discussion of the Barnum Effect (so named after the famous American showman, P.T. Barnum). In brief the Barnum Effect refers to a powerful tendency to believe information given to us about our personal qualities. This can be used to good effect by, for example, fortune tellers, astrologers, and handwriting 'experts'. If the 'expert' can say what people are prepared to accept, and can phrase it in such a way that it implies some intimate insight, then there is a good, if dishonourable, living to be made.

An early demonstration of this was provided by Forer (1949) in a classroom demonstration of gullibility. Forer described a personality test to his students and allowed them to persuade him to let them take the test (the first rule of a successful con is to appear reluctant!). Thirty-nine students completed the test. One week later, each was given a typed personality sketch with their name on it. The researcher encouraged the class to keep the results confidential, and the students were asked to indicate whether they thought the test results were accurate. In fact, they had been given identical personality sketches (see Table 5.2) which had no relationship to their test responses, yet all of the students rated the test as a perfect or near-perfect tool for investigating personality. This is a demonstration of the Barnum Effect. If we return to the study by Furnham and Varian (1988), we could argue that this is a demonstration of this same Barnum Effect, and that the EPI is successful, at least in part, because it provides plausible personality sketches.

Other problems with personality questionnaires

Kline (1993) identifies a number of sources of error in personality questionnaires, including:

1   acquiescence: people have a tendency to agree with items regardless of the content.
2   social desirability: people prefer to put themselves in a good light and so have a tendency to respond in a way that makes them appear all right. For example, we are unlikely to admit to only rarely washing even if that was true.
3   middle categories: many questionnaires ask people to respond on a five-point scale, and there is a tendency for people to use the middle value.

Personality tests are used extensively in occupational and clinical settings. A sophisticated technology has been developed to ensure the reliability of the tests and to produce evidence for their validity. Sometimes, however, the belief in the existence of certain behavioural

Table 5.2	The statements used by Forer (1949) in his demonstration of the Barnum Effect
1	You have a great need for other people to like and admire you.
2	You have a tendency to be critical of yourself.
3	You have a great deal of unused capacity which you have not turned to your advantage.
4	While you have some personality weaknesses, you are generally able to compensate for them.
5	Your sexual adjustment has presented problems for you.
6	Disciplined and self-controlled outside, you tend to be worrisome and insecure inside.
7	At times you have serious doubts as to whether you have made the right decision or done the right thing.
8	You prefer a certain amount of change and variety and become dissatisfied when hemmed in by restrictions and limitations.
9	You pride yourself as an independent thinker and do not accept others' statements without satisfactory proof.
10	You have found it unwise to be too frank in revealing yourself to others.
11	At times you are extroverted, affable, sociable, while at other times you are introverted, wary and reserved.
12	Some of your aspirations tend to be pretty unrealistic.
13	Security is one of your major goals in life.

patterns or personality characteristics can be more powerful than the scientific evidence. For example, the study of coping has been dominated by the Folkman and Lazarus (1990) description of coping styles (see Table 5.3). Their eight distinct styles of coping were derived from factor analysis, and their model is extensively applied and extensively researched on. A close look at the data, however, reveals that the eight coping styles are not as distinct as Folkman and Lazarus suggest, and it would be a more accurate reading of the data to take about only four or five factors (see Coyne and Gottlieb, 1996, and Ferguson and Cox, 1997).

Table 5.3 The eight coping strategies identified by Folkman and Lazarus through factor analysis but challenged by Ferguson and Cox

Problem-focused strategies	
1	Confrontive coping
2	Planful problem solving
Emotion-focused strategies	
3	Distancing
4	Self-controlling
5	Seeking social support
6	Accepting responsibility
7	Escape-avoidance
8	Positive reappraisal

Summary

The focus of this book is to consider controversies in psychology so the above brief section on personality testing does just that. I have only been able to give a flavour of the rigor of test development and extensive use that is made of psychometric tests. The enduring controversies include:

- labelling: is it appropriate to reduce a person's personality to a simple numerical index?
- stability of personality characteristics: even if we can obtain an accurate measure of a person's personality, does the result reflect their enduring personality characteristics or just how they were feeling when they took the test?
- validity: do the tests measure what they claim to measure, and in particular, has factor analysis given us descriptions of real personality variables or are they just statistical inventions?
- inheritance: how much of the differences in personality characteristics can be accounted for by genetics?
- Barnum Effect: are we gullible to the words of experts and can we put a lot of the effectiveness of personality tests down to this effect?

Design a psychometric test to measure stupidity (not necessarily the opposite of intelligence) or charmingness.

- Identify five items for the test
- Describe how you will assess the reliability of the test
- Suggest how you might assess the validity of the test

Further reading

Gould, S.J. (1981) *The Mismeasure of Man*, Harmondsworth: Penguin. A classic text that goes through the ways that psychologists have attempted to measure intelligence.

Kline, P. (1993) *Intelligence: The Psychometric View*, London: Routledge. A clear and concise account of the psychometric view of intelligence.

Study aids

IMPROVING YOUR ESSAY WRITING SKILLS

At this point in the book you have acquired the knowledge necessary to tackle the exam itself. Answering exam questions is a skill which this chapter shows you how to improve. Examiners have some ideas about what goes wrong in exams. Most importantly, students do not provide the kind of evidence the examiner is looking for. A grade C answer is typically accurate but has limited detail and commentary, and it is reasonably constructed. To lift such an answer to a grade A or B may require no more than fuller detail, better use of material and a coherent organisation. By studying the essays presented in this chapter, and the examiner's comments, you can learn how to turn grade C answers into grade A. Please note that marks given by the examiner in the practice essays should be used as a guide only and are not definitive. They represent the 'raw marks' given by an AEB examiner. That is, the marks the examiner would give to the examining board based on a total of 24 marks per question broken down into Skill A (description) and Skill B (evaluation). A table showing this scheme is in Appendix C of Paul Humphreys' title in this series, *Exam Success in AEB Psychology*. They may not be the marks given on the examination certificate received ultimately by the student because all examining boards are required to use a common standardised system called the Uniform Mark Scale (UMS) which adjusts all raw scores to a single standard acceptable to all examining boards.

The essays are about the length a student would be able to write in 35–40 minutes (leaving you extra time for planning and checking). Each essay is followed by detailed comments about its strengths and weaknesses. The most common problems to look out for are:

- Failure to answer the actual question set and presenting 'one written during your course'.
- A lack of evaluation, or commentary – many weak essays suffer from this.
- Too much evaluation and not enough description. Description is vital in demonstrating your knowledge and understanding of the selected topic.
- Writing 'everything you know' in the hope that something will get credit. Excellence is displayed through selectivity, and therefore improvements can often be made by removing material which is irrelevant to the question set.

For more ideas on how to write good essays you should consult *Exam Success in AEB Psychology* (Paul Humphreys) in this series.

Practice essay 1

Discuss why the assessment of personality and intelligence tests by means of psychometric tests might be considered controversial applications of psychology. (24 marks)

[AEB 1998]

Starting point: The essay can be broken down into three smaller questions to answer:

(i) How has psychology attempted to measure personality and intelligence?

(ii) What are the positive arguments for measuring intelligence and personality?

(iii) What are the negative arguments?

Part (i) is description and Parts (ii) and (iii) are evaluation.

These are the issues that need to be addressed, and the answer needs to identify the areas of controversy and say why they are controversial.

Candidate's answer

There are several different psychometric tests, like motivational tests, aptitude tests, personality and intelligence tests and they can be used to see whether someone is suitable for a job, have they got the right attitude to do the job and not the right qualifications. These tests can also be used to see whether the people will work well with their colleagues.

Examiner's comments: A breathless start to the essay, and a novel (if not brave) use of punctuation. It is a good idea to write in sentences (which means using full stops) and also to use short sentences. The paragraph does give a range of possible psychometric tests and says what they might be used for.

All these tests are very controversial and are widely discussed it is not just the problem of the test itself it is who is going to have access to the information should it be freely available or only available to the future employer or only the person him/herself. The results may effect the person by lowering their expectations and this could lead to problems of depression is this right and justifiable?

Examiner's comments: The poor punctuation continues throughout the essay so I will have one more moan about it and then shut up. Please write in sentences. An important issue is raised in the paragraph, namely the control of information from psychometric tests. It is raised as a question which is a good way to introduce it.

Another problem is that the tests themselves may not be a true assessment of the person, there are many different factors to take into account such as gender, cultural background, true intelligence, how much education you have had. Francis Galton did a study on Victorians and found that the wealthy families were much more intelligent and this was hereditary. The people in the slums were stupid and this was also hereditary. The problem with this is that the rich people had more education so were more likely to be intelligent.

Examiner's comments: This paragraph identifies the problem of infer-ring ability by testing performance. The writer, however, does not state this problem very clearly and goes on to make some alarming and only partially true assertions about Galton. It is always best to use technical terms in essays and, surprisingly enough, 'stupid', is not a technical term. On the other hand, it is worth knowing that 'moron', 'imbecile', 'cretin' and 'idiot' are, in fact, technical terms used by the early intelli-gence testers. This paragraph also gives the first outing to the author's rather simplistic view of genetic influences on performance.

Cultural issues are very difficult to rule out and cross-cultural psychometric tests are very hard to be bias free. One study showed that a Rail Attendants test at Paddington Station was biased against male Asians so many were not employed unfairly.

Examiner's comments: Cultural bias is certainly one of the important issues in psychometric testing, and the writer has illustrated the point with a badly remembered study.

Many tests are eurocentric and so are bias towards the White male middle class American or European. So if the test like this it is unlikely to be favourable to people who don't fit this bracket.

Examiner's comments: The term 'Eurocentric' means that the tests are constructed within the context of European ideas, attitudes and skills. It does not have anything to do with class or gender. Those are other sources of possible bias in tests.

It seems every test has a problem not to be bias even GCSE's can be bias because the British Government lays out guidelines for the syllabuses leading sometimes to controversies.

Examiner's comments: This is another reasonable point, but it could be developed much further by identifying the actual problem or by identi-fying the controversy.

There are a few tests that have been developed such as the Wheschler test – this has problems because it is more of a social conformity test rather than an intelligence test. Another two tests are the Alice Heim test and the British Ability Scale which by the name implies applies only to British people. Tests can also have problems discriminating about gender, some tests were done and it was found that women and girls were doing overall better than men and boys, so the results were changes so that women and girls had to get better results for the same mark. This is what they wanted to do for black people and applications of tests is this fair?

Examiner's comments: The writer correctly identifies another two tests but seems to know little more than the names of the tests. The point about adjustments to norms based on gender is appropriate though it is poorly developed.

What do you do with the results of the psychometric tests this could lead at the worst possible scenario to Eugenics and what Hitler did – trying to eradicate a race.

Examiner's comments: Adolf Hitler must be one of the most commonly cited people in psychology essays. The point is neither well made nor developed. The argument is this; if psychometric tests can be shown to measure ability rather than performance, and if differences between groups of people can be confidently identified and measured, and if these differences can be attributed to genetic influences rather than environmental ones, then it would suggest that selective breeding (eugenics) might be favoured by some people. There are a lot of 'ifs' in this argument and at least some of them need identifying in the essay.

There are two types of intelligence fluid which is innate and genetic and chrystalised which contains part of the fluid intelligence but is mainly to do with the environment. Is there a need for a complete classification of personality and intelligence? For employment it is useful so a lot of time and money is not spent on training someone who is not suitable for the job. Other areas of use which are personal will remain in discussion.

Examiner's comments: The first point is partially true and marginally relevant. The second point about the need for testing is a little more relevant but does not directly address the question.

Overall the writer shows a reasonable amount of psychological knowledge and identifies a few of the controversial issues around psychometric testing. Unfortunately, the knowledge is a little sparse and the points are only developed quite weakly. The expression is also quite weak. The final mark for this question is about 7(description) + 6(evaluation)=13/24 (likely to be equivalent to a grade C at A level).

Practice essay 2

Critically consider applications of psychological research to advertising. (24 marks)   [AEB 1998]

Starting point: The term 'critically consider' means the same as 'discuss'. The question can be broken down into three smaller questions that can be used to give structure to your answer,

(i)   How has psychology been used in advertising?
(ii) What are the benefits of the use of psychology in advertising?
(iii) What is the down side of using psychology in advertising?

Part (i) is description and Parts (ii) and (iii) evaluation.

Candidate's answer

Advertising is the means by which the ordinary public is persuaded to buy products or services. The way in which psychological research has aided this process is often thought of as being inhumane as it can invade people's thought and attitudes and then convince them into a different belief.

Advertising is targeted to people everywhere. It can include television, billboards, magazines adverts etc. As this information is bombarded into our senses it is believed that it is processed at a very low consciousness. This would mean that our attitudes could be changed without realising it.

Examiner's comments: Good introduction that defines some terms and introduces some of the possible areas of controversy.

An attitude can be changed by this theory which includes three stages:-

a) Cognitive component – your mood and feelings are changed about a product
b) Affective component – whether your thoughts about a product is changed
c) Behavioural component – this decides whether you go out and buy the product

Hedges believes that advertisements should have the following criteria in order to persuade people to buy,

1   A sense of familiarity and association
2   Rational argument in which to engage the customer in
3   Information
4   A mood or feeling.

Examiner's comments: The answer introduces two psychological frameworks that can be used to analyse advertisements. The first one is not a theory, by the way, but it is a useful way of looking at all sorts of human activity. The best thing to do after introducing these frameworks is to follow them through and apply them to some advertisements and comment on them.

Many advertisements use symbolic communication (Cannon and Cooper). This is where an advertisement targets part of the population e.g. the upper class, and the product shown is associated by this. For example 'After Eight' dinner mints are the only mints good enough for a particular dinner party. This inflicts social pressure and conformity on to those who do not like or cannot afford such things. It may in some cases be thought of as deviant. This is the great influence of advertising in people's lives.

Adverts for children's toys are often put on during children's programmes. Psychological research has found that buying is increased because children want what is shown to them. This is possibly because at school they have peer group pressure and have to have the commodities which are seen as 'cool'.

Examiner's comments: There are some missed opportunities here to score points by mentioning psychological concepts and research studies. The answer could have made more of social conformity, imitation, and the effects of the peer group. It is possible to attach the names of psychologists to these terms and also some key research studies. These names and studies will get you points, and remember, points win prizes!

One major controversy in advertising is the use of subliminal messages. This is when a picture/message is flashed on to a screen and the audience processes it without even noticing.

A study was performed during a cinema film where 'eat more popcorn, drink more Cola' was flashed up. The sales of these products increased. This study is however dubious because the title of the film was 'Picnic' so this may have been a confounding variable.

Examiner's comments: This is another good point that is partially remembered. The information is accurate, however, and the point about the confounding variable is a good one.

Psychologists have found that in the brain the right hemisphere deals with moods, feelings, attitudes. Many adverts therefore target this side of the brain to be more effective.

Another study was also performed where the music tempo in a supermarket was reduced and quickened. It was found that people bought more when the music was slow and browsed more.

Producers found though that people had brand loyalty so it was difficult to introduce new products. To overcome this problem researchers found that 'fast marketing' worked. This allowed customers to sample new products before buying them.

Researchers also found that the people in the advertisement who was trying to sell the product also mattered. For example, people would buy skin products if it was sold by a scientist (actor dressed in a white coat) or by a celebrity.

Examiner's comments: The strength of this essay is the range of material that is introduced. The weakness is that very little of it is presented in enough detail or developed as much as it could be. All the above four points are appropriate to the essay, but all of them could have been attached to a psychologist and described in a little more detail.

All these methods by which advertisements convince people to buy are mostly unknown by the consumers. It can therefore be seen as manipulating behaviour without consent. Adverts can persuade people to buy without knowing it has happened, or by making people to conform to what is seen as 'proper' in society and by making a product be desirable when it is not actually needed.

People however still have free thought and can choose what they wish.

In conclusion, however, I believe that after taking into account psychological methods, the above statement is not true and advertising is an invasion of one's privacy.

Examiner's comments: The answer draws to a conclusion by summarising the key points and making a final assessment of the evidence. The good part of this is that the essay has a nice shape in that it has a beginning (defining the terms and introducing the debate), a middle (the evidence) and an end (the concluding remarks). The down side is that the evidence is not described fully enough and the evaluation is not developed as far as it might be. The final mark for this question is around 8(description) + 6(evaluation)=14/24 (likely to be just about equivalent to a grade B at A level).

KEY RESEARCH SUMMARY

Article 1

'College sophomores in the laboratory: Influences of a narrow data base on psychology's view of human nature', D.O. Sears in *Journal of Personality and Social Psychology* (1986) 51, 513–30.

Who are psychology's subjects?

This study illustrates the sampling bias that exists within psychology, and challenges the conclusions that are often drawn from psychological research. At the heart of this is a very simple question: who are the people on whom psychological research is conducted, and can we generalise our results to all other people?

Sears carried out a thorough analysis of psychological research published in books and journals. For the basis of this summary we will look at just one part of the data which is shown in Table 6.1.

This shows that four-fifths of research used students as subjects, and most of the research was carried out in psychology laboratories. The questions now is, does this matter? Can we generalise from students to other people? Or, to put it another way, are there any differences between students and adults?

You can probably identify a number of differences yourself. Sears suggested that college students are not very representative of the general population. They come from a narrow age range and are predominantly at the upper levels of educational background and

Table 6.1 Subject populations and research sites in social psychology articles in 1985 (data shown in percentages)	
Subject population	% of articles
American undergraduates	
(a) Psychology classes	51
(b) Other classes	23
Other students	8
Total students	82
Adults	17
Research Site	
Laboratory	78
Natural habitat	22

income. The 17–19-year-old young people who make up the majority of subjects in psychology studies have been shown to have a number of unique characteristics which Sears summarised as follows:

(a) their self-concept is unlikely to be fully formed;
(b) social and political attitudes are less crystallised than in later life;
(c) they are more egocentric than elder adults;
(d) they have a stronger need for peer approval;
(e) they have unstable peer relationships.

Also, college students differ systematically from other people of the same age:

(f) they are pre-selected for competence at cognitive skills;
(g) they are selected for compliance to authority;
(h) their social and geographical mobility leads to enhanced instability in peer relationships.

This review suggests that some of the main findings of social psychology can only be applied to students and not to the general population.

Article 2

'Black is beautiful: a re-examination of racial preference and identification', J. Hraba and G. Grant in *Journal of Personality and Social Psychology* (1970) 16, 398–402.

Measuring racial identity

It is very difficult to measure what we think about ourselves, and what our identity is. This study used a simple but effective method of finding out what children identify with. The study by Hraba and Grant was a replication of work first carried out by Clark and Clark in 1939. They were interested in how racial awareness developed, and devised a novel test using dolls with different skin colour. Clark and Clark (1947) found that Black children preferred White dolls and rejected Black dolls when asked to choose which were nice, which looked bad, which they would like to play with, and which were a nice colour. This suggested that Black children had negative attitudes towards themselves and their cultural background. The studies were replicated a number of times over the next twenty years with similar results.

The studies have to be seen in a historical context. In America during the 1930s, many states had policies of segregation, and Black people were kept out of White areas and denied access to education, housing, welfare and jobs. The 1960s saw the growth of the civil rights movement (most famously under the leadership of Martin Luther King) and the growth of militant Black religious and political organisations (most famously that led by Malcolm X). This led to some improvement in the opportunities for Black people, and a change in the expectations of Black people. Since that time, Black people have made advances within American society and occupy an important place in the democratic structure. Despite this, the majority of Black people are still economically disadvantaged and the object of considerable racism.

The study

The children were interviewed individually using a set of four dolls: two Black and two White, but identical in all other respects. The children were asked to respond to a number of requests, and the ones that related to racial identity are the following:

1   Give me the doll that you want to play with
2   Give me the doll that is a nice doll
3   Give me the doll that looks bad
4   Give me the doll that is a nice colour

The subjects were 89 Black children and 71 White children aged between 4 and 8 years who attended primary schools in Lincoln, Nebraska, which was a predominantly White town.

RESULTS   The results provided a comparison of Hraba and Grant's data with that of Clark and Clark, and they also provide a comparison of the responses of Black children and White children.

Table 6.2 shows that, in the Lincoln study, Black and White children preferred the doll of their own 'race'. The White children were significantly more ethnocentric on items 1 and 2, there was no difference on item 3 and the Black children were significantly more ethnocentric on item 4. The Clarks had found that Black children preferred White dolls at all ages, though this decreased with age. Hraba and Grant found that Black children at all ages preferred a Black doll and this preference increased with age.

DISCUSSION   The results give a very different picture of doll preference in 1969 from doll preference in 1939. Hraba and Grant suggested a number of explanations for this discrepancy, but whichever interpretation you accept, this replication highlighted the fact that social psychological findings are inevitably the product of social climate in which they are conducted.

Table 6.2 Percentage responses to some of the doll questions

Item	Clark and Clark (1939) Black children	Lincoln study (1969) Black children	Lincoln study (1969) White children
1	'Play with'		
White doll	67	30	83
Black doll	32	70	16
don't know/no response			1
2	'Nice doll'		
White doll	59	46	70
Black doll	38	54	30
3	'Looks bad'		
White doll	17	61	34
Black doll	59	36	63
don't know/no response		3	3
4	'Nice colour'		
White doll	60	31	48
Black doll	38	69	49
don't know/no response			3

Glossary

The first occurrence of each of these terms is highlighted in **bold** type in the main text.

ability What a person is capable of, inferred through tests of performance.

ability tests Psychometric tests designed to measure what someone is already able to do, as opposed to what they might be able to learn in the future.

Acquired Immune Deficiency Syndrome (AIDS) AIDS is an infectious disease, most likely caused by a virus, that attacks the immune system making the host vulnerable to a variety of diseases that would be readily controlled by a healthy immune system.

affective To do with feelings or emotions, such as the component of an attitude concerned with feelings.

aggression A term used in several ways, but generally to describe negative or hostile behaviour or feelings towards others.

attitude A relatively stable opinion towards a person, object or activity, containing a cognitive element (perceptions and beliefs) and an emotional element (positive or negative feelings).

attribution The process of giving reasons for why things happen.

attribution theory The explanation of social perception by examining how people allocate intention or meaning to the behaviour of others.

authoritarian personality A collection of characteristics found by Adorno to occur together, implying a rigid approach to moral and social issues.

Barnum Effect Describes the fact that a carefully worded description of an individual's personality will often be uncritically accepted as valid if it presented in sufficiently broad and general terms.

behaviour shaping A process whereby novel behaviour can be produced through operant conditioning, by selectively reinforcing naturally occurring variations of learned responses.

behaviour therapy The process of treating abnormal behaviour by looking only at the symptoms, and using conditioning techniques to modify them.

behaviourism A reductionist school of thought which holds that the observation and description of overt behaviour is all that is needed to comprehend the human being, and that manipulation of stimulus–response contingencies is all that is needed to change human behaviour. In other words, behaviourism consists of denying the relevance or importance of cognitive, personal or other dimensions of human experience.

categorisation The first stage in the process of social identification, which involves grouping other people into social categories or sets. Research shows that such categorisation in itself, even if based on minimal criteria, can lead to a strong bias in favour of the in-group.

classical conditioning A form of learning which involves the pairing of a neutral stimulus with a reflex.

Coefficient Alpha (Cronbach's Alpha) A statistic which is used to give an estimate of reliability.

cognition Mental processes. Cognition includes the processes of perception, memory, thinking, reasoning, language and some types of learning.

cognitive dissonance The tension produced by cognitive imbalance, holding beliefs which directly contradict one another or contradict behaviour. The reduction of cognitive dissonance has been shown to be a factor in some forms of attitude change.

colonialism Political oppression where one nation or culture dominates another one, and in particular, removes wealth from the dominated culture, believes it has a right of access into the dominated culture, and has a power base outside the dominated culture.

compliance The process of going along with other people – i.e. conforming – but without accepting their views on a personal level.

concurrent validity A method for assessing whether a psychometric test is valid (i.e. really measures what it is supposed to) by comparing it with some other measure which has been taken at the same time (i.e. which is occurring concurrently).

conformity The process of going along with other people, i.e. acting in the same way that they do.

confounding variable A variable which causes a change in the dependent variable, but which is not the independent variable of the study.

construct validity A method for assessing whether a psychometric test is valid (i.e. really measures what it is supposed to) by seeing how it matches up with theoretical ideas about what it is supposed to be measuring.

control group A group which is used for comparison with an experimental group.

coping The process of managing external or internal demands that are perceived as taxing or exceeding a person's resource.

correlation A measure of how strongly two, or more, variables are related to each other.

correlation coefficient A number between -1 and $+1$ which expresses how strong a correlation is. If this number is close to 0, there is no real connection between the two; if it is close to $+1$ there is a positive correlation (in other words, if one variable is large the other will also tend to be large); and if it is close to -1, there is a negative correlation (in other words, if one variable is large, the other will tend to be small).

criterion validity A method for assessing whether a psychometric test is valid (i.e. really measures what it is supposed to) by comparing it with some other measure. If the other measure is assessed at roughly the same time as the original one, then the type of criterion validity being applied is concurrent validity; if it is taken much later, it is predictive validity.

cross-cultural studies Studies which examine psychological phenomonena in people from more than one cultural background.

cultural deprivation A construct which has been used to explain educational failure among members of certain classes.

demand characteristics Those aspects of a psychological study (or other artificial situation) which exert an implicit pressure on people to act in ways that are expected of them.

denial A coping strategy/Freudian defence mechanism where distressing facts are eliminated.

dependent variable The thing which is measured in an experiment, and which changes, depending on the independent variable.

discrimination The behavioural expression of prejudice.

dispositional attribution When the cause of a particular behaviour is thought to have resulted from the person's own personality or characteristics, rather than from the demands of circumstances.

dissonance See cognitive dissonance.

DSM–IV Published in 1994, it is the fourth edition of the *Diagnostic and Statistical Manual of Mental Disorders* developed by the American Psychiatric Association.

ecological validity A way of assessing how valid a measure or test is (i.e. whether it really measures what it is supposed to measure) which is concerned with whether the measure or test is really like its counterpart in the real, everyday world; in other words, whether it is truly realistic or not.

effect size When psychologists detect significant differences in the performance of subjects in experimental conditions, they talk about having 'got an effect'. The bigger the differences, the bigger is the effect size.

egocentrism The tendency to see things from your own personal perspective to the exclusion of other possible perspectives.

ergonomists Psychologists who try to match machines to people.

ethics A set of rules designed to distinguish between right and wrong.

ethnocentrism A syndrome of behaviours; (a) a tendency to under-value the out-group's products, (b) an increased rejection and hostility towards out-group members, (c) a tendency to over-value the in-group's products, (d) an increased liking for in-group members (accompanied by pressures for conformity and group cohesion).

eugenics The political idea that the human race could be improved by eliminating 'undesirables' from the breeding stock, so that they cannot pass on their supposedly inferior genes. Some eugenicists advocate compulsory sterilisation, while others seem to prefer mass murder or genocide.

Eurocentric The tendency to view Europe as THE main culture in human societies and to negatively compare all other cultures to Europe.

evolution The development of bodily form and behaviour through the process of natural selection.

expectancy effect A label to describe the way in which one person can effect the behaviour of another person simply by having expectations of that person. For example, it may be the case that having low expectations of a child in school can actually contribute to that child performing poorly.

experiment A form of research in which variables are manipulated in order to discover cause and effect.

experimenter effects Unwanted influences in a psychological study which are produced, consciously or unconsciously, by the person carrying out the study.

extroversion A general tendency towards outgoing social behaviour.

Eysenck Personality Inventory A psychometric scale for measuring neuroticism and extraversion.

face validity Whether a test or measure looks on the surface as though it probably measures what it is supposed to.

factoids 'Facts which have no existence before appearing in a magazine or newspaper' (Norman Mailer, cited in Pratkanis and Aronson, 1992, page 71).

factor analysis A method of statistical analysis which examines inter-correlations between data in order to identify major clusters of groupings, which might be related to a single common factor.

feedback Knowledge about the effectiveness of one's performance on a task or set of tasks. Feedback appears to be essential in most forms of learning, and is more effective if it is immediate.

feminist research Mary Gergen (1988) suggested the following as the main themes of feminist research: (1) recognising the interdependence of experimenter and subject; (2) avoiding the decontextualisation of the subject or experimenter from their social or historical surroundings; (3) recognising and revealing the nature of one's values within the research context; (4) accepting that facts do not exist independently of their producer's linguistic codes; (5) demystifying the role of the scientist and establishing an egalitarian relationship between science makers and science consumers.

g The abbreviation for 'general intelligence': a kind of intelligence which is supposed to underpin all different types of mental operations, as opposed to more specific types of talents or aptitudes; also a spot.

gender The inner sense of being either male or female.

genetic Biological inheritance.

group In psychology, usually more than two individuals.

heritability This statistic estimates how much the variation within any given population is due to genetic factors.

Human Immunodeficiency Virus (HIV) Human Immunodeficiency Virus is the virus that is believed to cause AIDS by attacking the immune system.

human nature The behavioural characteristics that define our species

identity The sense that you have of the sort of person you are.

imitation Copying someone else's behaviour and specific actions.

imitation effect A term used in consumer psychology to describe when a relatively small number of people adopt a new product, accept it and make it fashionable, then are imitated by others.

implicit racism Unconscious bias that comes out in judgements or actions.

independent variable The conditions which an experimenter sets up, to cause an effect in an experiment. These vary systematically, so that the experimenter can draw conclusions about changes.

inference Going beyond what we know to make an intelligent guess.

in-group A group you define yourself as belonging to.

innate Genetically pre-programmed.

Intelligence Quotient (IQ) A numerical figure, believed by some to indicate the level of a person's intelligence, and by others to indicate how well that person performs on intelligence tests.

intelligence An inferred characteristic of an individual, usually defined as the ability to profit from experience, acquire knowledge, think abstractly, or adapt to changes in the environment.

Interaction effect The result of at least two independent variables operating simultaneously on subjects' behaviour.

intergroup rivalry Competition between different social groups, which can often lead to powerful hostility.

internal attribution The judgement that a behaviour or act is caused by sources within the person – i.e. their character, personality or intentions. This is also known as dispositional attribution.

internal consistency If a test is internally consistent then the items in that test really are measuring the same thing (or same set of things). Note that this does not necessarily mean that they are measuring what they are meant to measure. In this respect internal consistency has more to do with reliability than validity.

interpersonal Literally 'between persons', this term is used to describe actions or occurrences which involve at least two people affecting one another in some way.

intra- As a prefix before any word this means 'within'.

learned helplessness The way that the experience of being forced into the role of passive victim in one situation can generalise to other situations, such that the person or animal makes no effort to help themselves in unpleasant situations even if such effort would be effective.

learning A change in behaviour, or the potential for behaviour, that occurs as a result of environmental experience, but is not the result of such factors as fatigue, drugs or injury.

learning theory The behaviourist approach that sees all learning in terms of classical and operant conditioning.

Likert scale Widely used in questionnaire studies and attitude surveys as the means by which subjects give 'ratings' in response to closed questions. The scale can be any size (often it is from 1–5 or 1–7), and each point on the scale is assigned a verbal designation. For example, on an attitude survey using a five-point Likert scale a rating of one might represent 'strongly agree', a rating of five might equal 'strongly disagree', a rating of three might equal 'neither agree nor disagree', and so forth.

minimal group paradigm An approach to the study of social identification which involves creating artificial groups in the social psychology laboratory on the basic of spurious or minimal characteristics (e.g. tossing a coin), and then studying the in-group/out-group effects which result.

moral development The development of moral reasoning in children and adults concerning judgments of what is 'right' and what is 'wrong'.

nature–nurture debates Fairly pointless theoretical debates, popular in the 1950s, concerning whether a given psychological ability was inherited or whether it was learned through experience.

neoteny The extension of childhood that has developed through evolution

obedience Complying to the demands of others, usually those in positions of authority.

operant conditioning The process of learning identified by B.F. Skinner, in which learning occurs as a result of positive or negative reinforcement of an animal or human being's action.

opinions Commonly used as a synonym for attitudes.

out-group A group you define yourself as NOT belonging to.

peer group A group of people who are considered to be the equals of, or like, the person concerned.

people of colour A term used (mainly in the United States) to refer to people who are not white and European. It is used to include people from Asia, and Hispanics as well as black people.

perception The process by which the brain organises and interprets sensory information.

performance The variable that is measured by psychometric tests, and which is used to infer **ability**, which is what you are capable of

personality A distinctive and relatively stable pattern of behaviours, thoughts, motives and emotions that characterise an individual.

personality type A simple of classification of people into narrow stereotypes, for example extrovert.

population In the context of research methods in psychology this refers to the total set of potential observations from which a sample is drawn.

population norms A set of scores for a particular population (e.g. females aged 18–24) which establishes the normal range of scores for that population, on a particular psychometric test or measure. Tables of population norms are used to judge whether an individual's test result is typical for their population group or not.

post-traumatic stress disorder An anxiety disorder resulting from experience with a catastrophic event beyond the normal range of human suffering, and characterised by (a) numbness to the world, (b) reliving the trauma in dreams and memories, and (c) symptoms of anxiety.

predictive validity A method of assessing whether a psychometric test is valid (i.e. really measures what it is supposed to) by seeing how well it correlates with some other measure, which is assessed later, after the test has been taken.

prejudice A fixed, preset attitude, usually negative and hostile, and usually applied to members of a particular social category.

propaganda Information designed to change feelings and beliefs (see Table 2.1)

psychology The scientific study of experience and behaviour. Psychology draws together systematic studies of experience and behaviour using a wide range of methods, and focusing on many different angles and levels of experience.

psychometric tests Instruments which have been developed for measuring mental characteristics. Psychological tests have been developed to measure a wide range of things, including creativity, job attitudes and skills, brain damage, and, of course, 'intelligence'.

qualitative data Data which describe meaning and experience rather than providing numerical values for behaviour such as frequency counts.

race Commonly used to refer to groups of people such as white people or black people, etc. It implies a genetic component to the differences between these groups, but research shows that the term 'race' has no biological validity, and is best described as a political construct.

racism Using the pervasive power imbalance between races/people to oppress dominated peoples by devaluing their experience, behaviour and aspirations.

random sample A way of selecting a sample where every person from the defined population has an equal chance of being chosen.

reactivity A term used to describe the way in which the behaviour of research subjects can be affected by some aspect of the research procedure. Most commonly it is used to describe the way in which the behaviour of someone who is being observed is affected by the knowledge that they are being observed.

reinforcement Anything that increases the probability that a behaviour will recur in similar circumstances. The term is usually used of learned associations, acquired through operant or classical conditioning, but it may also be applied to other forms of learning.

reliability The reliability of a psychological measuring device (such as a test or a scale) is the extent to which it gives consistent measurements. The greater the consistency of measurement, the greater the tool's reliability.

repression A coping strategy in which a person forces unwanted thoughts or feelings out of their conscious awareness into their unconscious.

retrieval cues small pieces of information that can trigger the recall of events or substantial amounts of material.

role A social part that one plays in society.

sample The group of subjects used in a study: the selection of people, animals, plants or objects drawn from a population for the purposes of studying that population.

scientific racism The use of bogus scientific arguments to enhance the power of one group of people over another.

self-concept The idea or internal image that people have of what they themselves are like, including both evaluative and descriptive dimensions.

self-efficacy beliefs The belief that one is capable of doing something effectively. Self-efficacy beliefs are closely connected with self-esteem, in that having a sense of being capable and potentially in control tends to increase confidence. But the concept is often thought to be more useful than the generalised concept of self-esteem, since people may often be confident about some abilities, or in some areas of their lives, but not in others.

self-esteem The evaluative dimension of the self-concept, which is to do with how worthwhile and/or confident the person feels about themself.

self-fulfilling prophecy The idea that expectations about a person or group can become true simply because they have been stated.

self-report A number of popular research methods are based on self report; for example, questionnaires, interviews, attitude scales and diary methods. These are methods which rely on research subjects' accounts of their own experiences and behaviour.

sensory deprivation The cutting out of all incoming sensory information, or at least as much of it as possible.

sex differences A large body of psychological research exists which documents differences between females and males.

sexism Using the pervasive power imbalance between men and women to oppress women by devaluing their experience, behaviour and aspirations.

siblings Brothers and sisters.

simulation A method of investigation where the participants act out a particular scene or pattern of behaviours.

situational attribution A reason for an act or behaviour which implies that it occurred as a result of the situation or circumstances that the person was in at the time.

sleeper effect In the first instance, people are affected by the source of amessage rather than the content, but over time the source of the message is forgotten and the content becomes more important.

social norms Socially or culturally accepted standards of behaviour, which have become accepted as representing how people 'ought' to act and what is 'normal' (i.e. appropriate) for a given situation.

sociobiology The attempt to explain social behaviour within an evolutionary context. It relies heavily for evidence on ants, and obscure species with unusual characteristics such as the Blue Bollocked Gibbon of Goa.

standard deviation A measure of dispersion.

standardisation (a) The process of making sure that the conditions of a psychological study or psychometric test are always identical; (b) the process of establishing how the results of a psychometric test will usually come out in a given population, by drawing up sets of population norms; (c) the process of comparing a new psychometric test with older, more established measures of the same thing.

stimulus An external environmental event to which an organism responds.

subliminal perception The registration and processing of sensory information below the level of consciousness awareness.

test–retest method A system for judging how reliable a psychometric test or measure is which involves administering the same test to the same people on two different occasions, and comparing the results.

trait A specific facet of personality.

unconscious mind The part of our mind that is beyond our conscious awareness.

validity The question of whether a psychometric test or psychological measure is really measuring what it is suppose to.

variability hypothesis Simply, this suggests that the range of scores for men on a number of psychological measures is wider than the range of scores for women.

war What is it good for, HUH! The organisation of groups of people, often nations, to attack other groups of people for reasons of domination, control of territory or control of resources.

Bibliography

Ackoff, R.L. and Emshoff, J.R. (1975) Advertising research at Anheuser-Busch, Inc., *Sloan Management Review* 16, 1–15.

Adorno, T.W., Frenkel-Brunswik, G., Levinson, D.J. and Sanford, R.N. (1950) *The Authoritarian Personality*, New York: Harper.

Archibald, H.C.D., Long, D.M., Miller, C. and Tuddenham, R.D. (1963) Gross stress reactions in combat, *American Journal of Psychiatry* 119, 317.

Asch, S.E. (1955) Opinions and social pressure, *Scientific American* 193, 31–5.

Atkinson, R.L., Atkinson, R.C., Smith, E.E., Bem, D.J. and Hilgard, E.J. (1990) *Introduction to Psychology*, 10th edn, San Diego, CA: Harcourt Brace Jovanovich.

Azibo, D.A.ya (ed.) (1996) *African Psychology in Historical Perspective and Related Commentary*, Trenton, NJ: Africa World Press.

Baggaley, J. (1991) Media health campaigns: not just what you say, but the way you say it, in World Health Organisation, *AIDS Prevention Through Health Promotion: Facing Sensitive Issues*, Geneva: World Health Organisation, 24–32.

Baron, R.A. and Byrne, D. (1991) *Social Psychology: Understanding Human Interactions*, 6th edn, Boston: Allyn & Bacon.

Bekerian, D.A. and Baddeley, A.D. (1980), Saturation advertising and the repetition effect, *Journal of Verbal Learning and Verbal Behaviour* 19, 17–25.

Bramson, L. and Geothals, G.W. (eds) (1968) *War: Studies from Psychology, Sociology and Anthropology*, revised edn, New York: Basic Books.

Brean, H. (1958) What hidden sell is all about, *Life*, 31 March, 104–14.

Broverman, I.K., Broverman, D.M. and Clarkson, F.E. (1971) Sex-role stereotypes and clinical judgements of mental health, *Journal of Consulting and Clinical Psychiatry* 34, 1–7.

Cattell, R.B. and Butcher, H.J. (1968) *The Prediction of Achievement and Creativity*, Indianapolis, IN: Bobbs-Merrill.

Chaiken, S. and Eagly, A.H. (1983) Communication modality as a determinant of persuasion: the role of communicator silence, *Journal of Personality and Social Psychology* 45, 241–56.

Cohen, D. (1979) *J.B. Watson: The Founder of Behaviourism*, London: Routledge.

Coyne, J. and Gottlieb, B. (1996) The mismeasure of coping by check-list, *Journal of Personality* 64, 959–91.

Dawkins, R. (1976) *The Selfish Gene*, Harmondsworth: Penguin.

Deaux, K. (1984) From individual difference to social categories: analysis of a decade's research on gender, *American Psychologist* 39, 105–16.

Durbin, E.F.M. and Bowbly, J. (1938), in L. Bramson and G.W. Geothals (eds), *War: Studies from Psychology, Sociology and Anthropology*, revised edn, New York: Basic Books, 1968, 81–104.

Eagle, R. (1980) Why are politicians so charismatic, *New Scientist* 2 October, 33–35

Earley, P.C. (1989) Social loafing and collectivism: a comparison of United States and the People's Republic of China, *Administrative Science Quarterly* 34, 565–81.

Ehrlich, D., Guttman, I., Schonback, P. and Mills, J. (1957) Postdecision exposure to relevant information, *Journal of Abnormal and Social Psychology* 54, 98–102.

Elliot, J. (1984) How advertising on milk bottles increased consumption of Kellogg's Corn Flakes, in S. Broadbent (ed.), *Twenty Advertising Case Histories*, London: Holt, Rinehart, Winston, 228–36.

Engel, J.F., Blackwell, R.D. and Miniard, P.W. (1990) *Consumer Behaviour*, 6th edn, Chicago: The Dryden Press.

Eysenck, H.J. (1947) *Dimensions of Personality*, London: Routledge & Kegan Paul.

Ferguson, E. and Cox, T. (1997) The functional dimensions of coping scale: Theory, reliability and validity, *British Journal of Health Psychology* 2, 109–29.

Festinger, L. (1957) *A Theory of Cognitive Dissonance*, New York: Harper and Row.

Flynn, J. (1990) Explanation, evaluation and a rejoinder to Rushton, *The Psychologist* 5, 199–200.

Folkman, S. and Lazarus, R. (1990) Coping and emotion, in A. Monat and R. Lazarus, *Stress and Coping*, 3rd edn, New York: Columbia University Press.

Forer, B.R. (1949) The fallacy of personal validation: a classroom demonstration of gullibility, *Journal of Abnormal and Social Psychology* 44, 118–21.

Fox, S. (1984) *The Mirror Makers*, New York: William Morrow.

Freud, S. ([1933]1985) 'Why War?', in *Pelican Freud Library*, vol. 12, pp. 349-62.

—— ([1933]1973) *The New Introductory Lectures on Psychoanalysis*, Harmondsworth: Penguin.

Furnham, A. and Varian, C. (1988) Predicting and accepting personality test scores, *Personality and Individual Differences* 9, 735–48.

Furumoto, L. and Scarborough, E. (1992) Placing women in the history of psychology: the first American women psychologists, in J.S. Bohan (ed.), *Seldom Seen, Rarely Heard: Women's Place in Psychology*, Boulder, CO: Westview, 337–53.

Gilligan, C. and Attanucci, J. (1988) Two moral orientations: gender differences and similarities, *Merrill Palmer Quarterly* 34, 223–37.

Gilovich, T. (1981) Seeing the past in the present: the effects of associations to familiar events on judgements and decisions, *Journal of Personality and Social Psychology* 40, 797–808.

Gould, S.J. (1978) Women's brains, *New Scientist* 2 November, 364–6.

—— (1981) *The Mismeasure of Man*, Harmondsworth: Penguin.

—— (1982) A nation of morons, *New Scientist* 6 May, 349–52.

Gregory, W and Burroughs, W. (1989) *Applied Psychology*, Glenview, IL: Scott Foresman.

Haney, C., Banks, C. and Zimbardo, P. (1973) A study of prisoners and guards in a simulated prison, *Naval Research Review* 30, 4–17.

Hayes, N. (1995) *Psychology in Perspective*, London: Macmillan.

Hearnshaw, L. (1979) *Cyril Burt, Psychologist*, Ithaca, NY: Cornell University Press.

Heather, N. (1976) *Radical Perspectives in Psychology*, London: Methuen.

Herrnstein, R.J. (1973) *I.Q. in the Meritocracy*, London: Allen Lane.

Hewstone, M., Stroebe, W., Codol, J.P. and Stephenson, G. (1988) *Introduction to Social Psychology: A European Perspective*, Oxford: Blackwell.

Hitler, A. (1925) *Mein Kampf*, trans. E.T.S. Dugdale, Cambridge, MA: Riverside.

Hodgkinson. P.E. and Stewart, M. (1991) *Coping with Catastrophe*, London: Routledge.

Horowitz, I.A. and Kaye, R.S. (1975) Perception and advertising, *Journal of Advertising Research* 15, 15–21.

Hovland, C.I., Janis, I.L. and Kelly, H.H. (1953) *Communication and Persuasion*, New Haven, CT: Yale University Press.

Hovland, C.I., Lumsdaine, A.A. and Sheffield, F.D. (1949) *Studies in Social Psychology in World War II*, vol. 3, *Experiments in Mass Communication*, Princeton, NJ: Princeton University Press.

Howitt, D. (1991) *Concerning Psychology: Psychology Applied to Social Issues*, Milton Keynes: Open University Press.

Hunt, N. (1997) Trauma of war, *The Psychologist* 10, 357–60.

James, W. (1910) The moral equivalent of war, in L. Bramson and G.W. Geothals (eds), *War: Studies from Psychology, Sociology and Anthropology*, revised edn, New York: Basic Books, 1968, 21–31.

Janis, I. and Feshbach, S. (1953) Effects of fear-arousing communications, *Journal of Abnormal and Social Psychology* 48, 78–92.

Jones, J.M. (1991) Psychological models of race: what have they been and what should they be? in J.D. Goodchilds (ed.), *Psychological Perspectives on Human Diversity in America*, Washington: American Psychological Association, 3–45.

Kamin, L.J. (1977) *The Science and Politics of IQ*, Harmondsworth: Penguin.

Kapferer, J.N. (1989) A mass poisoning rumour in Europe, *Public Opinion Quarterly* 53,. 467–81.

Kaplan, R.M. and Saccuzzo, D.P. (1993) *Psychological Testing: Principles, Applications and Issues*, Pacific Grove, CA: Brooks/Cole.

Keller, K.L. (1987) Memory factors in advertising: the effect of advertising retrieval cues on brand evaluations, *Journal of Consumer Research* 14, 316–33.

Kitzinger, C. (1998) Challenging gender biases: feminist psychology at work, *Psychology Review* 4. 18–20.

Kline, P. (1991a) *Intelligence: The Psychometric View*, London: Routledge.

—— (1993) *The Handbook of Psychological Testing*, London: Routledge.

Kohlberg, L. (1968) The child as a moral philosopher: psychology today, in D. Krebs (ed.), *Readings in Social Psychology*, 2nd edn, London: Harper Collins, 1968.

Lashley, K. and Watson, J.B. (1921) A psychological study of motion pictures in relation to venereal disease, *Social Hygiene* 7, 181–219.

Latané, B., Williams, K. and Harkins, S. (1979) Many hands make light the work: causes and consequences of social loafing, *Journal of Personality and Social Psychology* 37, 822–32.

LeVine, R.A. and Campbell, D.T. (1972) *Ethnocentrism: Theories of Conflict, Ethnic Attitudes and Group Behaviour*, New York: Wiley.

Lindzey, G. and Aronson, E. (1985) *Handbook of Social Psychology*, 3rd edn, New York: Random House, vol. 2.

Lifton, R.J. (1961) *Thought Reform and the Psychology of Totalism: A Study of 'Brainwashing' in China*, London: Victor Gollancz.

Maccoby, E.E. and Jacklin, C. (1974) *The Psychology of Sex Differences*, Stanford, CA: Stanford University Press.

MaCullough, M. (1988) Are we secret racists? *The Psychologist* 3, 445–7.

Manheim, J.B. (1993) The war of images: strategic communication in the gulf conflict, in S. Renshon (ed.), *The Political Psychology of the Gulf War*, Pittsburgh, PA: Pittsburgh University Press, 155–79.

Mark, L.S., Warm, J.S. and Huston, R.L. (1987) *Ergonomics and Human Factors: Recent Research*, New York: Springer-Verlag.

Mathur, M. and Chattopadhyay, A. (1991) The impact of moods generated by television programs on responses to advertising, *Psychology and Marketing* 8, 59–77.

Matsumoto, D. (1994) *People: Psychology From a Cultural Perspective*, Pacific Grove, CA: Brooks/Cole.

McCrae, R.R. and Costa, P.T., Jr (1985) Updating Norman's 'adequate taxonomy': intelligence and personality dimensions in natural language and in questionnaires, *Journal of Personality and Social Psychology* 49, 710–21.

McDougall, W. (1915) *An Introduction to Social Psychology*, London: Methuen.

McGuire, W.J. (1964) Inducing resistance to persuasion: some contemporary approaches, in L. Berkowitz (ed.), *Advances in Experimental Social Psychology*, vol. 1, New York: Academic Press.

—— (1973) Persuasion, resistance and attitude change, in I. Pool *et al.* (eds), *Handbook of Communication*, Skokie, IL: Rand McNally, 216–52.

—— (1985) Attitudes and attitude change, in G. Lindzey and E. Aronson (eds), *Handbook of Social Psychology*, New York: Random House.

Mead, M. (1940) Warfare is only an invention – not a biological necessity, in L. Bramson and G.W. Geothals (eds), *War: Studies from Psychology, Sociology and Anthropology*, revised edn, New York: Basic Books, 1968, 269 – 74.

Milgram, S. (1963) Behavioural study of obedience, *Journal of Abnormal and Social Psychology* 67, 371–78.

Miller, G. (1969) Psychology as a means of promoting human welfare. *American Psychologist* 24, 1063–75.

Milliman, R. (1982) Using background music to affect the behaviour of supermarket shoppers, *Journal of Marketing* 46, 86–91.

Moghaddam, F.M., Taylor, D.M. and Wright, S.C. (1993) *Social Psychology in Cross-Cultural Perspective*, New York: W.H. Freeman.

Mullen, B. and Johnson, C. (1990) *The Psychology of Consumer Behaviour*, New Jersey: Lawrence Erlbaum Associates.

Myers, J.H. and Reynolds, W.H. (1967) *Consumer Behaviour and Marketing Management*, Boston, MA: Houghton-Mifflin.

Nobles, W. (1976) Extended self: rethinking the so-called Negro self-concept, *Journal of Black Psychology* 2, 15–24.

Olney, T.J., Holbrook, M.B. and Batra, R. (1991) Consumer responses to advertising: the effects of ad content, emotions and attitude towards the ad on viewing time, *Journal of Consumer Research* 17, 440–51.

Orne, M.T. (1962) On the social psychology of the psychological experiment: with particular reference to demand characteristics and their implications, *American Psychologist* 17, 776–83.

Pendergrast, M. (1993) *For God, Country and Coca-Cola*, London: Weidenfeld.

Petty, R.E., Cacioppo, J.T. and Schumann, D. (1983) Central and peripheral routes to advertising effectiveness: the moderating role of involvement, *Journal of Consumer Research* 10, 134–48.

Pilger, J. (1975) *The Last Day*, London: Mirror Group Books.

—— (1989) *Heroes*, London: Pan.

Pratkanis, A.R. and Aronson, E. (1992) *Age of Propaganda: The Everyday Use and Abuse of Persuasion*, New York: W.H. Freeman.

Pratkanis. A.R., Greenwald, A.G., Leippe, M.R. and Baumgardner, M.H. (1988) In search of reliable persuasion effects: III. The sleeper effect is dead. Long live the sleeper effect, *Journal of Personality and Social Psychology* 54, 203–18.

Qualls, W.J. and Moore, D.J. (1990) 'Stereotyping' effects on consumers' evaluation of advertising: effects of racial differences between actors and viewed, *Psychology and Marketing* 7, 135–51.

Reardon, K.K. (1991) *Persuasion in Practice*, London: Sage.

Renshon, S.A. (ed.) (1993) *The Political Psychology of the Gulf War*, Pittsburgh: Pittsburgh University Press.

Richards, G. (1998) The case of psychology and 'race', *The Psychologist* 11, 179–81.

Ries, A. and Trout, J. (1981) *Positioning: The Battle for Your Mind*, New York: McGraw-Hill.

Rose, S., Kamin, L.J. and Lewontin, R.C. (1984) *Not in Our Genes*, Harmondsworth: Penguin.

Rosenthal, R. and Jacobson, L. (1968) Teachers' expectancies: deter-minates of pupils' I.Q. gains, *Psychological Reports* 19, 115–18.

Rushton, J., (1990) Race differences, r/K theory and a reply to Flynn, *The Psychologist* 5, 195–98.

Schrank, J. (1977) *Snap, Crackle and Popular Taste*, New York: Dell.

Sears, D. (1986) College sophomores in the laboratory: influences of a narrow data base on psychology's view of human nature, *Journal of Personality and Social Psychology* 51, 515–30.

Seaver, W.B. (1973) The effects of naturally induced teacher expectancies, *Journal of Personality and Social Psychology* 28, 333–42.

Shallice, T. (1973) The Ulster depth interrogation techniques and their relation to SD research, *Cognitive Psychology* 1.

Sherif, M. (1956) Experiments in group conflict, *Scientific American* 195, 54–8.

Shevlin, M.E. (1995) An exploratory and theoretical examination of measurement: reliability, assessment and control, Ph.D. thesis, University of Ulster.

Shevlin, M.E. and Miles, J. (1998) Cronbach's Alpha: not always a lower-bound estimate of reliability, *Northern Ireland Branch of the British Psychological Society*, Carricart, Co. Donegal.

Shields, S. (1978) Sex and the biased scientist, *New Scientist* 7 December, 752–4.

Shils, E.A. and Janowitz, M. (1948) The impact of propaganda on Wehrmacht solidarity, in H. Brown and R. Stevens (eds), *Social Behaviour and Experience: Multiple Perspectives*, London: Hodder & Stoughton, 1975.

Shotter, J. (1975) *Images of Man in Psychological Research*, London: Methuen.

Sigel, R.S. (1964) Effect of partisanship on the perception of political candidates, *Public Opinion Quarterly* 28, 488–96.

Skinner, B.F. (1960) Pigeons in a pelican, *American Psychologist* 15, 28–37.

—— (1972) *Beyond Freedom and Dignity*, Harmondsworth: Penguin.

Smith, P.B. and Bond, M.H. (1993) *Social Psychology Across Cultures: Analysis and Perspectives*, London: Harvester Wheatsheaf.

Soden, M. and Stewart, M. (1984) The repositioning of Lucozade, in S. Broadbent (ed.), *Twenty Advertising Case Histories*, Eastbourne: Holt, Rinehart, Winston.

Stayman, D.R. and Batra, R. (1991) Encoding and retrieval of as affects in memory, *Journal of Marketing Research* 28, 232–9.

Storr, A. (1968) *Human Aggression*, Harmondsworth: Penguin.

Swank, R. (1949) Combat exhaustion, *Journal of Nervous and Mental Disorders* 9, 369–76.

Tajfel, H. (1970) Experiments in intergroup discrimination, *Scientific American* 223, 96–102.

Tavris, C. (1991) The mismeasure of woman: paradoxes and perspectives in the study of gender, in J.D. Goodchilds (ed.), *Psychological Perspectives on Human Diversity in America*, Washington, DC: American Psychological Association, 87–135.

Taylor, A.J.P. (1963) *The First World War: An Illustrated History*, Harmondsworth: Penguin.

Thompson, G.E. (1984) Post-it notes click thanks to entrepreneurial spirit, *Marketing News* 18, 21–3.

Thompson, J. (1985) *Psychological Aspects of Nuclear War*, Leicester: BPS Books.

Turnbull, C.M. (1961) *The Forest People*, New York: Simon & Schuster.

Watson, J.B. (1913) Psychology as the behaviourist views it, *Psychological Review* 20, 158–78.

—— (1930) *Behaviourism*, revised edn, New York: Harpers.

Watson, P. (1980) *War on the Mind: The Military Uses and Abuses of Psychology*, London: Penguin.

Waugh, M.J. (1997) Keeping the home fires burning, *The Psychologist* 10, 361–3.

Wayne, S.J. (1993) President Bush goes to war: a psychological interpretation from a distance, in S. Renshon (ed.), *The Political Psychology of the Gulf War*, Pittsburgh: Pittsburgh University Press, 29–47.

Weisstein, N. (1992) Psychology constructs the female, or the fantasy life of the male psychologist (with some attention to the fantasies of his friends the male biologist and the male anthropologist), in J.S. Bohan (ed.), *Seldom Seen, Rarely Heard: Women's Place in Psychology*, Boulder, CO: Westview, 61–78.

White, H. (1980) Name change to Rusty Jones helps polish product's identity, *Advertising Age* 18 February, 47–8.

Williams, J.H. (1987) *Psychology of Women*, 3rd edn, New York: Norton.

Wilson, E.O. (1975) *Sociobiology: The New Synthesis*, Cambridge, MA: Harvard University Press.

Windle, C. and Vallance, T (1964) The future of military psychology: paramilitary psychology, *American Psychologist* 19.

Zimbardo, P.G. and Leippe, M.R. (1991) *The Psychology of Attitude Change and Social Influence*, New York: McGraw-Hill.

Index

163